Frommer's

Banff & the Canadian Rockies
day BY day

2nd Edition

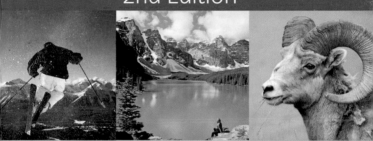

by Christie Pashby

Contents

Published by:

John Wiley & Sons, Inc.

111 River St.
Hoboken, NJ 07030-5774

ISBN 978-1-118-42218-2 (paper); 978-1-118-50143-6 (ebk);
978-1-118-50142-9 (ebk)

Editor: Gene Shannon
Production Editors: Michael Brumitt, Lindsay Conner
Photo Editor: Alden Gewirtz
Cartographer: Andrew Murphy
Production by Wiley Indianapolis Composition Services

Front cover photos: *Left:* © Gary Pearl / StockShot / Alamy Images.
Middle: © Imagebroker / Thomas Sbampato Alamy Images.
Right: © George Ostertag / SuperStock / Alamy Images.

Back cover photo: © Rolf Hicker Photography / Alamy Images.

For information on our other products and services or to obtain technical
support, please contact our Customer Care Department within the U.S.
at 877/762-2974, outside the U.S. at 317/572-3993 or fax 317/572-4002.

Wiley also publishes its books in a variety of electronic formats. Some
content that appears in print may not be available in electronic formats.

Manufactured in China

5   4   3   2   1

Letter from the Editorial Director

Organizing your time. That's what this guide is all about.

Other guides give you long lists of things to see and do and then expect you to fit the pieces together. The Day by Day guides are different. These guides tell you the best of everything, and then they show you how to see it *in the smartest, most time-efficient way*. Our authors have designed detailed itineraries organized by time, neighborhood, or special interest. And each tour comes with a bulleted map that takes you from stop to stop.

Hoping to spot animals in the wild or hike through beautiful alpine meadows? Planning to stay in an authentic mountain lodge or soak in an outdoor hot springs? Whatever your interest or schedule, the Day by Days give you the smartest routes to follow. Not only do we take you to the top attractions, hotels, and restaurants, but we also help you access those special moments that locals get to experience—those "finds" that turn tourists into travelers.

The Day by Days are also your top choice if you're looking for one complete guide for all your travel needs. The best hotels and restaurants for every budget, the greatest shopping values, the wildest nightlife—it's all here.

Why should you trust our judgment? Because our authors personally visit each place they write about. They're an independent lot who say what they think and would never include places they wouldn't recommend to their best friends. They're also open to suggestions from readers. If you'd like to contact them, please send your comments our way at feedback@frommers.com, and we'll pass them on.

Enjoy your Day by Day guide—the most helpful travel companion you can buy. And have the trip of a lifetime.

Warm regards,

Kelly Regan

Kelly Regan, Editorial Director
Frommer's Travel Guides

About the Author

Christie Pashby has written for Frommer's for nearly a decade, contributing to titles including *Frommer's Argentina, Frommer's Chile,* and *Best Hikes in British Columbia.* She divides her time between the Canadian Rockies and Bariloche, Argentina. A freelance journalist and translator, she also somehow finds the time to run a small guiding business with her husband, and cram in two ski seasons a year. Her website is www.patagonialiving.com.

Acknowledgments

I'd like to thank my congenial editor Gene Shannon, as well as the staff at Travel Alberta and the Banff Lake Louise Tourism Bureau.

Advisory & Disclaimer

Travel information can change quickly and unexpectedly, and we strongly advise you to confirm important details locally before traveling, including information on visas, health and safety, traffic and transport, accommodations, shopping, and eating out. We also encourage you to stay alert while traveling and to remain aware of your surroundings. Avoid civil disturbances, and keep a close eye on cameras, purses, wallets, and other valuables.

While we have endeavored to ensure that the information contained within this guide is accurate and up-to-date at the time of publication, we make no representations or warranties with respect to the accuracy or completeness of the contents of this work and specifically disclaim all warranties, including without limitation warranties of fitness for a particular purpose. We accept no responsibility or liability for any inaccuracy or errors or omissions, or for any inconvenience, loss, damage, costs, or expenses of any nature whatsoever incurred or suffered by anyone as a result of any advice or information contained in this guide.

The inclusion of a company, organization, or website in this guide as a service provider and/or potential source of further information does not mean that we endorse them or the information they provide. Be aware that information provided through some websites may be unreliable and can change without notice. Neither the publisher nor author shall be liable for any damages arising herefrom.

Star Ratings, Icons & Abbreviations

Every hotel, restaurant, and attraction listing in this guide has been ranked for quality, value, service, amenities, and special features using a **star-rating system.** Hotels, restaurants, attractions, shopping, and nightlife are rated on a scale of zero stars (recommended) to three stars (exceptional). In addition to the star-rating system, we also use a **kids icon** to point out the best bets for families. Within each tour, we recommend cafes, bars, or restaurants where you can take a break. Each of these stops appears in a shaded box marked with a coffee-cup-shaped bullet 🍵 .

The following **abbreviations** are used for credit cards:

AE	American Express	DISC	Discover	V	Visa
DC	Diners Club	MC	MasterCard		

Travel Resources at Frommers.com

Frommer's travel resources don't end with this guide. Frommer's website, **www.frommers.com**, has travel information on more than 4,000 destinations. We update features regularly, giving you access to the most current trip-planning information and the best airfare, lodging, and car-rental bargains. You can also listen to podcasts, connect with other Frommers.com members through our active-reader forums, share your travel photos, read blogs from guidebook editors and fellow travelers, and much more.

A Note on Prices

In the "Take a Break" and "Best Bets" sections of this book, we have used a system of dollar signs to show a range of costs for 1 night in a hotel (the price of a double-occupancy room) or the cost of an entree at a restaurant. Use the following table to decipher the dollar signs:

Cost	Hotels	Restaurants
$	under $100	under $10
$$	$100–$200	$10–$20
$$$	$200–$300	$20–$30
$$$$	$300–$400	$30–$40
$$$$$	over $400	over $40

How to Contact Us

In researching this book, we discovered many wonderful places—hotels, restaurants, shops, and more. We're sure you'll find others. Please tell us about them, so we can share the information with your fellow travelers in upcoming editions. If you were disappointed with a recommendation, we'd love to know that, too. Please write to:

Frommer's Banff & the Canadian Rockies Day by Day, 2nd Edition
John Wiley & Sons, Inc. • 111 River St. • Hoboken, NJ 07030-5774
frommersfeedback@wiley.com

18 Favorite
Moments

18 Favorite **Moments**

Legend:

- Gasoline
- Hospital/First Aid
- (i) Information
- Point of Interest
- Skiing

1. Gazing at the peaks from the top of Sulphur Mountain
2. Skiing the Great Divide at Sunshine Village
3. Fly-fishing on the Upper Bow River
4. Exploring an ice castle on a starry winter's night
5. Catching live jazz at the Banff Centre
6. Skating on a frozen lake
7. Hiking or cross-country skiing into Skoki Lodge
8. Hiking Lake O'Hara Alpine Circuit
9. Viewing Saskatchewan Glacier from Parker Ridge
10. Sunday brunch at the Fairmont Banff Springs
11. Soaking in the Banff Upper Hot Springs on a winter evening
12. Tea at the Plain of the Six Glaciers
13. Wildflowers at Healy Pass
14. Morning coffee run
15. Catching your first wildlife sighting
16. Setting up a mountain picnic
17. Driving the astonishing Icefields Parkway
18. Canoeing on an alpine lake

Previous page: A hiker admires the scenery along the Lake O'Hara Alpine Circuit.

Banff has been drawing visitors to the Canadian Rocky Mountains for more than a century. They're drawn primarily to nature and the peace of the wilderness. It's not necessarily hip (although Banff has trendy restaurants), and it's certainly nothing new. Banff is dependable yet surprising, a place to stretch yourself physically and reward yourself mentally. The following are some of my favorite experiences in Canada's premier mountain wilderness.

❶ Gazing at the peaks from the top of Sulphur Mountain. It's the easiest summit in the Canadian Rockies. Take the 8-minute gondola ride to the top of Sulphur Mountain, and then walk the elevated 1km (⅔-mile) boardwalk to Sanson Peak, a truly jaw-dropping lookout. Six mountain ranges are displayed beneath you. Also great for families, this is an easy way to accomplish a kid's first Rocky Mountain summit. Hard-core hikers can hike up the 5.3km (3.3-mile) switchback trail and then reward their knees by riding the gondola down. *See p 13,* **❷**.

❷ Skiing the Great Divide at Sunshine Village. On a perfect winter day, catch the Continental Divide chair up to the top of Lookout Mountain, crossing from Alberta into British Columbia en route. The view of Mt. Assiniboine, the "Matterhorn

of the Rockies," is magnificent, and when the powder is fresh and the sun is shining, your ski back down will be even more thrilling. *See p 43, Day 5.*

❸ Fly-fishing on the Upper Bow River. Slow things down by heading downriver from the Town of Banff on the clear and pristine Upper Bow to try your luck at hooking a brown, brook, or rainbow trout. Remember, it's strictly catch and release, and you must have a permit from Parks Canada. In Jasper, the trout gather on the Maligne River. Since the best fishing often happens on the lousiest days, this is a great rainy-day outing. *See p 153.*

❹ Exploring an ice castle on a starry winter's night. Late January brings the annual Ice Magic event to the frozen shores of Lake

Sulphur Mountain's peak can be accessed easily by gondola or vigorously on foot.

Fly-fishing on the Upper Bow River.

Louise. Under the dark sky and beneath the icy glaciers of Mt. Victoria, carvers from around the world craft magical creations, culminating with a frozen castle that stays on the lake as long as the water is frozen. Rent some skates at the Fairmont Chateau Lake Louise, snuggle by the outdoor fire, and sip hot chocolate—the ingredients of a midwinter's dream come true. *See p 160.*

❺ Catching live jazz at the Banff Centre. Year-round concerts at this globally renowned arts and cultural center bring in some of the sharpest musicians from around the world. During the summer, the Banff Summer Arts Festival also showcases dance, opera, theater, and literary journalism. An inspiring way to spend the evening! *See p 55.*

❻ Skating on a frozen lake. Clear as glass on a crisp winter day, the shallow Vermillion Lakes, close to the Town of Banff, make for a magical ice rink. The crisp mountain views and glimpses of fish wintering below the ice add to the icy drama. What could be more Canadian? Just be sure to check ice thickness with Parks Canada first. In Jasper, try Pyramid Lake. *See p 41,* ❸.

❼ Hiking or cross-country skiing into Skoki Lodge. This historic cabin tucked in the woods behind Lake Louise Ski Resort may be the place that defined rustic mountain charm. The 11km (6.8-mile) trail leads to a wooden cabin with private rooms, home cooking, endless trails—and no electricity or running water. It's like stepping back in time to a pure and unspoiled mountain retreat. *See p 82.*

❽ Hiking the Lake O'Hara Alpine Circuit. Just the word "O'Hara" brings oohs and aahs from veteran hikers. Across the British Columbia border behind Lake Louise, in Yoho National Park, this is an exquisite hiking destination, dotted with meadows, lookouts, ridgewalks, turquoise lakes, and meticulously chiseled stone trails. There are a half-dozen superb hikes to choose from, but the Alpine Circuit highlights the best of the best. Remember to book your bus ride up to the lake in advance. *See p 25.*

❾ Viewing the Saskatchewan Glacier from Parker Ridge. Hike for just over an hour for views even more stunning than those you can see from your car on the

The crystal clear surface of Lake O'Hara in Yoho National Park.

The alpine wildflowers at Healy Pass are picture-perfect in July and August.

Icefields Parkway. The trail starts steeply, but soon plateaus out into the subalpine zone, offering gorgeous views of the Saskatchewan Glacier and Mt. Athabasca. Don't forget to look down and around you too—you may see fossils, rosy finches, mountain goats, and maybe even a grizzly bear. For solitude and spectacular vistas, few short hikes in the world can compare. *See p 46,* **7**.

10 Sunday brunch at the Fairmont Banff Springs. In the stately Bow Valley Grill inside this legendary hotel, you can sample a stellar array of gourmet Canadiana, from smoked Wild Pacific salmon and free-range eggs Benedict, to roasted Alberta beef and maple brownies. Ask for a window table for views of the Fairholme Range and Bow River, and bring your appetite. Reservations recommended. *See p 14,* **3**.

11 Soaking in the Banff Upper Hot Springs on a winter evening. If it's cold and you've been skiing all day, you're in the right town—just head to the historic bathhouse to relax in the natural hot pools (ranging from 99°–104°F/ 37°–40°C), open until 10pm weeknights in winter and 11pm on winter weekends. Other hot springs in the mountain parks worth visiting include Miette Hot Springs in Jasper National Park and the Radium Hot Springs in Kootenay National Park. *See p 14,* **7**.

12 Tea at the Plain of the Six Glaciers. Drawing hikers since 1924, this historic teahouse is a rustic cabin nestled in a gorgeous location at the back of Lake Louise. It's a 2-hour hike to get here—surely you deserve a piece of chocolate cake or banana loaf? Take your pot of tea and sit outside to marvel at the six glaciers that cling to Aberdeen, Lefroy, Victoria, and Popes Peak. *See p 146.*

13 Wildflowers at Healy Pass. In the high alpine zone, hardy wildflowers like moss Campion, purple Saxifrage, glacier lilies, and alpine forget-me-nots bloom into gorgeous colors from mid-July to mid-August. This pass just beside Sunshine Village ski area is one of the finest areas for these brilliant displays. Hike the 12km (7.5-mile) trail up to alpine meadows, or cheat by taking the Sunshine Meadows shuttle up most of the way. In Jasper, head to Mt. Edith Cavell. *See p 100,* **8**.

14 Morning coffee run. Early morning is the quietest time of the

Canoeing on a serene alpine lake.

day on the otherwise-bustling main strip of Banff Avenue. Before 9am, it's the peaceful terrain of locals. Join them for a cafe latte and whole-wheat waffles (served with apple maple sauce) at the Wild Flour Bakery. As the workers head off, relish your vacation time with a stroll along the Bow River. In Jasper, do the same at the Bear's Paw Bakery. *See p 127.*

⑮ Catching your first wildlife sighting. Whether it's an elk munching on grass on a lawn or a grizzly bear crossing an avalanche path, each glimpse of a wild animal in Banff is a gift. There are no guarantees, but there's a good chance that you'll see bighorn sheep at Lake Minnewanka at dusk or dawn. Some animals, of course, require more seriousness than others. Visit the Parks Canada Visitors Centre for more information. *See p 13,* ❶.

⑯ Setting up a mountain picnic. Quieter than the Trans-Canada Highway, the Bow Valley Parkway's best picnic spot is at the Storm Mt. Lookout, just north of Castle Junction, for great views and photo ops. Pick up supplies for a scrumptious picnic at the Bison Bistro's General Store in Banff or at Laggan's in Lake Louise. *See p 142.*

⑰ Driving the astonishing Icefields Parkway. For 230km (143 miles), drive a road that feels like it's been carved inside the earth, with massive mountains clinging to the Continental Divide, ancient glaciers, and ragged peaks. At the middle is the Columbia Icefield, the liquid heart from which the waters of the nation pump. Oh, and there are mountain goats and grizzly bears too! *See p 64.*

⑱ Canoeing on an alpine lake. Emerald, Maligne, Moraine, their names simply invite you to grab a paddle and launch a canoe upon their sublime shores. Out alone (or with a friend) on a placid alpine lake, with your reflection blending with that of giant rocky peaks on the ripples beside you, you'll find you're living inside your own postcard from paradise. Moraine Lake is next to Lake Louise and is less visited but still easy to access, making it my top choice. *See p 63,* ❾. ●

1 Strategies for Seeing **Banff & the Canadian Rockies**

Banff & the Canadian Rockies

Previous page: Photo opportunities can arise anywhere—even on the road between sites.

he beautiful Canadian Rockies are a vast area with so much to see and do. Your time is precious and you need to plan according to the seasons, the length of your visit, and your goals and tastes. Don't try to do it all—the magic in Banff is in the quietest moments. In this chapter I have several tips to help you make the most of your time.

Rule #1: Get out of town!

While the Town of Banff holds most of the lodgings and restaurants, not to mention shops and nightlife, it's what you'll find in the rest of the park that will most astound you. Those particularly interested in solitude should head to a nearby national park—Jasper in the north, or Kootenay and Yoho to the west—or to one of the many backcountry lodges dotted throughout the park. Even day trips in a car or a short hike count towards spreading your wings here.

Rule #2: Go to the experts and visit the Parks Canada Information Centres

These should be your first stop, whether it's in the Town of Banff, at Lake Louise, or in Jasper. Pick up maps and permits and take in interpretive exhibits that will greatly enhance your experience in the Canadian Rockies. The friendly staff members have the latest trail, road, avalanche, and wildlife reports, and can answer just about any question you have.

Rule #3: Don't over-schedule

Jam-packing your days from an early morning bird-watching trip to a late-night stargazing excursion will only leave you exhausted. The loveliest moments in Banff are those that surprise you—spotting a wolf on a quiet road, or having a leisurely picnic by the river. Give yourself time for spontaneous adventure and explorations.

Rule #4: Allow plenty of travel time

Not only are the distances great, but you'll find lots of mountains along the way that provide twists and turns—there are few straight lines in the Canadian Rockies. And along the way from A to B, there'll likely be dozens of photo opportunities and maybe even some wildlife sightings. Plan to get out of the car often, and take your time while driving.

Rule #5: Come in the shoulder season

Not only will it save you money, but you'll avoid the crowds. June is

The Lake Louise visitor centre provides maps, permits, and park information.

Mountains at every turn can make for winding roads and slow driving.

considered off season, and September (my favorite month in Banff) is great for hiking. For winter travelers, try pre-Christmas December for good deals and April for spring skiing.

Rule #6: Be prepared for weather

In the Rockies, it's common to see all four seasons in a day, any time of the year. Even in the middle of summer, don't be surprised to see snow—bring appropriate clothing and never hit the trail without a good jacket, sunscreen, and a bottle of water.

Rule #7: Try something new

Banff is a great place to do something you've never done before—or something you haven't done in years. Hiking

Carefree skiing in the off season.

isn't just for the super-fit and horseback riding ain't only for cowboys. The campground up at Lake O'Hara may be the most accessible backcountry camping in the mountains, so give it a try. In wintertime, take a snowboard lesson or try ice-skating. Vacations are for breaking free!

Rule #8: Pick one central activity each day and plan around it

For days when you plan to head out for a hike or hit the slopes, get ready the evening before. Pack food, get your gear ready, and check the latest conditions. And get a good night's sleep! Be logical so that you don't have to backtrack.

Rule #9: Think outside the park

Save cash by staying in a hotel just outside Banff. The Town of Canmore, just 20km (12 miles)—a 15-minute drive—east of Banff, is a lovely mountain town with an impressive list of affordable hotel options.

Rule #10: Use this book as a reference, not a concrete plan

Don't worry; I won't be hurt if you don't follow every single tour I lay out here. Read through the options I present, pick the ones that most appeal to you, and adapt them to your personal circumstances. ●

2

The Best
Full-Day Tours

Banff in Three Days

DAY 1

1. Banff Information Centre
2. Sulphur Mountain Gondola
3. Fairmont Banff Springs Hotel
4. Coyotes Grill
5. Tunnel Mountain
6. Bison Mountain Bistro
7. Upper Hot Springs

DAY 2

8. Lake Louise Village
9. Laggan's Mountain Deli
10. Lake Louise
11. Fairmont Chateau
    Lake Louise
12. Tea at the Chateau
13. Moraine Lake
14. Bow Valley Parkway

DAY 3

15. Crowfoot Glacier
16. Peyto Lake
17. Saskatchewan Crossing
18. Columbia Icefield
19. Columbia Glacier
    Icefield Experience

Gasoline

ⓘ Information

Point of Interest

Skiing

Previous page: Canoeing is a beautiful way to explore Banff's tranquil lakes.

Located at the confluence of the Spray and Bow rivers, and on the lower slopes of Tunnel and Sulphur mountains, the Town of Banff is rich in culture and history, with adventure at your doorstep. START: **Banff Information Centre, corner of Wolf Street and Bear Street.** TRIP LENGTH: **7km + 4.6km hike is 11.6km (7.2 miles).**

Travel Tip

Avoid parking hassles by using the ROAM hybrid bus system, which runs down all the routes mentioned below. An unlimited day pass costs $5. For more information, call ☎ 403/762-6770. Days 2 and 3 require your own vehicle.

The Sulphur Mountain Gondola.

Day 1

❶ ★★ Banff Information Centre. No visit to Banff should start anywhere else. Stock up on maps and free self-guided tour brochures, and get helpful advice from the knowledgeable and friendly staff of the Parks Canada, Banff/Lake Louise Tourism Bureau, and Friends of Banff desks. ⏲ *30 min. 224 Banff Ave.* ☎ *403/762-1550. Mid-May to mid–June 9am–7pm; mid-June to early Sept 8am–8pm; early through late Sept 9am–7pm; late Sept to mid-May 9am–5pm.*

Hop on the ROAM bus 1 or drive up Banff Avenue over the Bow River Bridge. Take a left after the bridge onto Spray Avenue and a quick right up Mountain Road until you arrive at:

❷ ★ kids Sulphur Mountain Gondola. A quick 8-minute gondola ride takes you to the top of this 2,285m (7,496 ft.) peak. Walk the elevated boardwalk to Samson Peak. Bring at least a sweater! ⏲ *60 min. At the end of Mountain Rd., 2.5km (1½ miles) from Banff Ave.*

The staff at the Banff Information Centre are knowledgeable and eager to help.

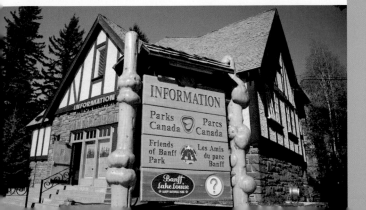

Nonguests can enjoy the Fairmont Banff Springs Hotel over a meal or short tour.

☎ 403/762-2523. Adults $30, kids 6 and up $15. Free for kids 5 and under. Jan 1–2 10am–4pm; Jan 24–Mar 30 8:30am–5pm; Mar 31–May 4 8:30am–6:30pm; May 5–Oct 21 8am–9pm; Oct 22–Dec 31 10am–5pm. Jan 3–13 closed for annual maintenance.

Head back down Mountain Road, taking a right at Spray Avenue. If you are on the ROAM bus 1, you'll have to change lines on to bus 2 at the corner of Spray Avenue and Mountain Road. Continue to the right until you arrive at:

③ ★★ Fairmont Banff Springs Hotel. Even if all you do is drive by, you can't miss the unmistakable stone towers and green roof of this national landmark. Ostentatious and oozing with amenities, it's an expensive place to stay (p 79), but a marvelous building and certainly a must-see on any trip to Banff. Nonguests are welcome to grab a meal or take a short tour of the hotel. ⏱ 45 min. 405 Spray Ave. ☎ 403/762-2211.

From the Banff Springs, head back down Banff Avenue into town. Turn left on Caribou Street to:

④ Lunch at Coyotes Grill. Few places have stood the test of time as well as this Southwest-inspired bistro in the heart of Banff. Run by devoted locals, the food is fresh and tasty. Try a corn-crusted pizza or chicken enchilada. 206 Caribou St. ☎ 403/762-3963. $$.

Leave the streets behind, walking up Wolf Street towards the Banff Centre, keeping an eye out for the trail head for:

⑤ ★★ Tunnel Mountain Hike. Work off lunch by hiking this classic Banff trail that heads right out of the heart of town. It's a 2.3km (1.4-mile) hike that takes you 300m (984 ft.) up to the lookout. One of the oldest trails in the park, this is very popular with Banff locals. ⏱ 2½ hr. Trail head is at St. Julien Rd., 300m (984 ft.) uphill from the Wolf St. junction.

Head back into town on Wolf Street, turning left on Bear Street. Half a block down, you'll find:

⑥ The Bison. Hit the sunny patio here for a treat. Overlooking Bear Street and Mt. Rundle, it's got the best view of any patio in town. Upscale cheese and meat trays make great appetizers, and there's a long wine-by-the-glass menu and local beers on tap. See p 71. 211 Bear St. ☎ 403/762-5550. $$.

After a leisurely meal, hop back on the ROAM bus 1 or drive up Mountain Road towards:

⑦ ★★ Upper Hot Springs. For more than a century, visitors have come to Banff to "take the waters." Evenings are the best time at these historic pools. ⏱ 60 min. At the end of Mountain Rd., 2.5km (1½ miles) from downtown Banff. ☎ 403/762-1515.

Mid-Oct to mid-May Sun–Thurs 10am–10pm, Fri–Sat 10am–11pm; mid-May to mid-Oct daily 9am–11pm. Adult $7.30, seniors and children (3–17) $6.30.

Day 2

Your day begins with a delightful 45-minute drive to Lake Louise. Head straight there from Banff—you'll have time later in the afternoon to look around the Bow Valley. Your goal is to beat the crowds to the lake and to secure the best light for taking photos. **START: From your hotel in the Town of Banff, take the Trans-Canada Highway west from the Mt. Norquay Road.**

1 ★ Lake Louise Village. A small "'hamlet" just off the Trans-Canada Highway, this is a collection of hotels, restaurants, gas stations, and shops, centered at the Samson Mall. Pick up a snack or grab a new fleece if the weather has soured. The Parks Canada Information Centre is just behind the shopping plaza, worth a visit for trail and wildlife updates. ⏱ *40 min. 58km (36 miles) west of the Town of Banff on Trans-Canada Hwy. 1.*

2 Laggan's Mountain Deli. This unpretentious coffee and sandwich shop is popular with hikers, bikers, skiers, and anybody on the move. It's in the middle of Samson Mall. Beat the crowds by entering the alternative door on the left side and heading for the second cashier. *101 Lake Louise Dr., in Samson Mall. ☎ 403/522-2017. $.*

Drive out of the Samson Mall parking lot onto Village Road, turning left at Lake Louise Drive and head up the hill until you reach:

3 ★★★ Lake Louise. Perhaps the most photographed lake in Canada, this stunner draws thousands of visitors every week from every corner of the globe. At the back of the lake, Mt. Victoria and the Victoria Glacier make an imposing backdrop. Take an hour to stroll to the back of the lake. Find a quiet spot for a snack.

It's impossible to miss the massive building to your right:

4 ★★ Fairmont Chateau Lake Louise. This landmark hotel is known as "'the diamond in the wilderness." For more than 115 years, mountaineers, artists, and lovers of the outdoors have been drawn to the sublime landscape outside of, and the grace inside of, this hotel. ⏱ *30 min. 111 Lake Louise Dr. ☎ 403/522-1818.*

5 Tea at the Chateau. If you're not a guest, you can experience the refined elegance of this famous hotel by reserving a table for afternoon tea in the Lakeview Lounge. By reservation only. *111 Lake Louise Dr. ☎ 403/522-1818. $$.*

Drive out of the parking lot and take the first right on the Moraine Lake Road, which leads you to:

6 ★★★ Moraine Lake. Some say Louise's less-visited sister lake is

Lake Louise attracts photographers from all around the world.

even more beautiful. Wild and dramatic, Moraine Lake is surrounded by 10 spire-like peaks. There's a great interpretive trail to the Moraine Lake Rockpile. ⏲ *45 min. 13km (8 miles) south of Lake Louise on Moraine Lake Road.*

Bid farewell to the Lake Louise area, driving back down to the village. Drive over the Trans-Canada Highway, taking the next right on to:

❼ Bow Valley Parkway 1A.

Built in 1920, the first road connecting Banff and Lake Louise still feels more like a mountain road than an expressway. Compared to the Trans-Canada Highway, the Parkway is quieter and gives you a much better chance for wildlife sightings.

The day ends returning on the Bow Valley Parkway 1A and then finally on the Trans-Canada Highway into the Town of Banff.

Day 3

One of the most beautiful drives in the entire world, a day on the icefield is not to be missed. Continuing north on the Icefields Parkway from Lake Louise, the road steadily climbs higher and higher and the views become more and more dramatic as you make your way through three river valleys and pass beneath towering glacier-

Dramatic Moraine Lake is surrounded by peaks.

topped peaks. Get an early start, as the first stop is over an hour from Banff. **START: From the Town of Banff head west on the Trans-Canada Highway. Just past Lake Louise, turn north on Hwy. 93 towards Jasper.**

Travel Tip

Food options are next-to-nonexistent once you pass Lake Louise, so pick up a picnic there or in Banff. You must have a valid Park Pass to drive on this highway. See p 59.

❶ ★ Crowfoot Glacier. The first

of a long lineup of glaciers you'll see once resembled the foot of a crow (hence the name), but has shrunk significantly. There are interpretive signs posted at the roadside viewpoint. ⏲ *10 min. 32km (20 miles) from Lake Louise on Hwy. 93, the Icefields Parkway.*

Continue north on the Icefields Parkway to:

❷ ★★ Peyto Lake. There is a

short interpretive trail to this beautiful turquoise gem, named for pioneer guide Bill Peyto, who was also a warden in Banff National Park. ⏲ *20 min. 42km (26 miles) from Lake Louise on Hwy. 93, the Icefields Pkwy.*

Continue north on the Icefields Parkway to:

❸ Saskatchewan Crossing.

This is the only place with any kind of services between Lake Louise and the Icefields Centre. Besides lovely views of the Mistaya, Howse, and North Saskatchewan river valleys, there is a warden station, gas station, snack bar, and gift shop. ⏲ *10 min. 50km (31 miles) from Lake Louise on Hwy. 93, the Icefields Pkwy.*

Crowfoot Glacier, one of the many breathtaking sights along the Icefields Parkway.

Continue north on the Icefields Parkway to:

❹ ★★★ Columbia Icefield.

Just north of the Banff–Jasper Park border, this is an area of glacial ice and snow measuring 190 sq. km (73 sq. miles) that is up to 350m (1,148 ft.) deep in places. It'll give you an idea what the northern part of North America may have looked like during the Earth's last ice age. There are six main glaciers flowing from the Columbia Icefield. Park at the Icefields Centre, the main building in the area. This is where you need to go to sign up for a tour on the snocoach. ⏱ *2–3 hr. total. 125km (78 miles) from Lake Louise on Hwy. 93, the Icefields Pkwy.* ☎ *780/852-6288. May 1 to mid-June and Sept 3 to mid-Oct daily 9am–5pm; mid-June to Sept 2 daily 9am–6pm; closed Oct 16–Apr 30.*

Directly across the highway is:

❺ ★★ kids The Columbia Glacier Icefield Experience.

Take a giant snocoach onto the Athabasca Glacier, which drops you off in the middle of the ice where you can walk around. Expect to have to wait for availability in tours, especially in July and August. Come early or late for shorter wait times. Tours leave every 15 minutes or so. ⏱ *90 min.* ☎ *403/762-6735. Adults $50, kids 6–15 $25. Apr 6–30 and Oct 1–18 10am–4pm; May 1–31 and Sept 1–30 9am–5pm; June 1–Aug 31 9am–6pm. 125km (78 miles) from Lake Louise on Hwy. 93, the Icefields Pkwy.*

The day ends retracing your steps back to Banff on Hwy. 93 and then on the Trans-Canada Hwy. 1.

The lookout onto Peyto Lake is a short hike away from Icefields Parkway.

Best in **One Week**

⛽	Gasoline
ℹ️	Information
⬛	Point of Interest

1 Town of Banff

2 Horseback riding at the Spray River

3 Lake Louise

4 Icefields Parkway

5 Hiking at Lake Louise

6 Yoho National Park

   6a Spiral Tunnels

   6b Takakkaw Falls

   6c Field

   6d Sidings General Store and Café

   6e Emerald Lake

   6f Cilantro on the Lake

7 Biking at Lake Louise

Having a few extra days allows you time to explore the backcountry of Banff National Park and visit the historically—and geographically—fascinating Yoho National Park, next door to Banff. You can blend both active adventures, like hiking and horseback riding, with traditional touring and sightseeing. START: **Town of Banff.**

Day 1
Follows the Town of Banff tour from Day 1 earlier.

Day 2
Saddle up today to head into the mountains. Follow in the steps of cowboys, pack guides, and wilderness explorers near Banff. **Holiday on Horseback's** Warner's Stables, which has run trail rides in Banff for nearly 50 years, has a full-day trip that heads up the Spray River and includes a barbecue lunch (p 154). *132 Banff Ave.* ☎ *800/661-8352 or 403/762-4551.*

Day 3
Today follows Day 2 of "Banff in Three Days" with one difference: Drive up to Lake Louise on the Bow Valley Parkway, stopping at Johnston Canyon and Muleshoe en route (p 59), and plan on spending the next few nights based out of Lake Louise.

Day 4
Today follows Day 3 of "Banff in Three Days," taking in all the highlights of the

Trail riding up the Spray River.

spectacular Icefields Parkway, returning to Lake Louise in the evening.

Day 5
Lake Louise hiking: In a land of superlatives, there are many outstanding hiking options to choose from. The classic Lake Louise hike, the Highline Trail, connects Lake Agnes with the Plain of the Six Glaciers, two historic teahouses, massive glaciers, and a lovely, gentle downhill finish. *Tip:* Pick up lunch supplies at Laggan's in Samson Mall, and be sure to bring plenty of water! *See Chapter 6 for trail descriptions.*

Day 6
Yoho National Park: "Yoho" is an expression of awe and wonder in the Cree language, and that's just what you'll experience in this park, located just over the provincial border from Banff in British Columbia. Yoho showcases the western slopes of the Rockies with dozens of spectacular waterfalls and the Kicking Horse River. It's also an interesting spot for history buffs. START: **Lake Louise.**

Take the Trans-Canada Hwy. 1 west from Lake Louise 9.2km (5¾ miles) to the border between Alberta and British Columbia. At 8.7km (5½ miles) west of the border, turn off into the roadside interpretive display at:

❶ ★ **Spiral Tunnels.** Steep as it is, the CPR (Canadian Pacific Railway) in the 1880s selected the Kicking Horse Pass as the easiest way over the Rockies. But it was still very, very steep, and soon enough trains were crashing down the so-called "Big Hill." The Spiral Tunnels

A train emerging from Cathedral Mountain through the Spiral Tunnels.

were designed more than 100 years ago to take trains through two loops inside Cathedral Mountain, easing the grade. View the Spiral Tunnels from the side of Trans-Canada Hwy. 1 just up the hill from Field; there are excellent interpretive signs, and if your timing's good, you'll actually catch a train going through the tunnels (on an average day, 25 to 30

Takakkaw Falls in Yoho National Park.

trains pass through the tunnels, though not on a regular schedule).

Continue down the hill on the Trans-Canada Highway another 3.7km (2¼ miles), turning right at Yoho Valley Road for:

❷ ★★ **Takakkaw Falls.** Reach the fourth-highest waterfall in Canada by driving up the Kicking Horse River on Yoho Valley Road (not recommended for large RVs or trailers). If you love waterfalls, you've come to the right place. Hike in another hour along the Yoho Valley trail past Staircase Falls and Point Lace Falls to see Laughing Falls and then on to beautiful Twin Falls.

Drive back out to the Trans-Canada Hwy. 1, continuing 1.8km (1 mile) west to the Field turnoff.

❸ ★ **Field.** With a population of only 200 souls, the tiny town of Field, BC, has a gorgeous setting beside the Kicking Horse River and beneath Mt. Stephen. There are a few charming shops, including the Velvet Antler Pottery ⏲ *30 min. (on Stephen Ave. next to Sidings Café,* ☎ *250/343-6456). 27km (17 miles) from Lake Louise.*

Cilantro on the Lake provides stunning alpine views in summertime.

Head through tiny Field, turning right on Kicking Horse Avenue, and make a quick U-turn at Stephen Avenue to find:

④ ★ Sidings General Store and Café.
A cozy deli in historic Field is a good stop any time of day: Arrive pre-hike for a breakfast sandwich or to get a "designer" sandwich to go. Or come by post-hike for a date square, brownie, and cup of tea. It's even open for dinner, with salads, pastas, and a great veggie chili. *318 Stephen Ave., at the corner of Kicking Horse Ave.* ☎ *250/343-6002. $$.*

Back out on the Trans-Canada Highway, turn left (west), and continue 2km (1¼ miles) to the turnoff for Emerald Lake Road. Drive 8km (5 miles) until you reach:

⑤ ★★ Emerald Lake.
Move past the crowded parking lot and hike the lovely 5km (3.1-mile) trail around this marvelous alpine lake. With just a little bit of up and down, this wide trail that circles the pristine Emerald Lake is rich and delightful, almost easy enough to be considered a stroll. Legendary local guide Tom Wilson is credited for having "discovered" this natural marvel in 1882 as part of a route-scouting for the Canadian

Pacific Railroad. This is a great family outing or leg-stretcher; it showcases a gem of a lake, and the interpretive signs are informative.

⑥ ★ Cilantro on the Lake.
Open only during the summertime (early June through mid-Sept), this is a pretty mountain bistro at Emerald Lake Lodge offering wood-fired flatbread pizzas, gourmet burgers, and microbrewed beer in a sublimely beautiful setting. Sit on the lovely, sunny patio overlooking Emerald Lake or inside the spectacular timber-frame lodge. *On Emerald Lake Rd., 8km (5 miles) off Trans-Canada Hwy., at a turnoff 2km (1¼ miles) south of Field.* ☎ *250/343-6321. $$.*

Day 7
Your final day is for some morning adventure. Rent a mountain bike from **Wilson Mountain Sports** in Samson Mall (from $15/hour or $39/day; ☎ 866/929-3636 or 403/522-2178) and ride the 9km (5.6-mile) return classic Tramline Trail. Families will prefer the gentle Bow River Loop or the Great Divide Bike Path, which is better suited to a road bike. Then give yourself plenty of time to say goodbye to the Rockies and head out.

The Best Full-Day Tours

Best in **Two Weeks**

ucky are those with time to linger in the Canadian Rockies. After all, there are nearly 23,000 sq. km (8,880 sq. miles) of mountain wilderness to explore, and that takes time. Blending sight-seeing with active adventures, and allowing you to roam from Banff up to Jasper, this is perhaps the ultimate 2-week vacation in this inimitable setting. Just be sure to book ahead of time, particularly your night at Yoho National Park's Lake O'Hara—either at the camp-ground or the historic and peerless Lake O'Hara Lodge. For more details see p 137.

Day 1
See Day 1 from the "Banff in Three Days" tour, p 13.

Day 2
Aim to hit the trail today on horse-back. See Day 2 of "Best in 1 Week," p 19.

Day 3
★★ kids **Sunshine Meadows.**
When the snow melts at the world-famous Sunshine Village ski area, the alpine meadows blossom into a multicolored dreamland hugging the Continental Divide, great for moder-ate hiking amid more than 340 spe-cies of wildflowers. The Garden Path Trail is breathtaking in late July and August. To the south you can see Mt. Assiniboine, the "Matterhorn of the Rockies." Take a bus from the parking lot or right from the Town of Banff and skip the arduous uphill hike. *Tip:* Book the morning buses ahead of time, and don't forget to bring a lunch, bear spray, and

drinking water, and use plenty of sun-screen. *8km (5 miles) west of Banff on the Sunshine Rd.* ☎ *403/762-7889. $26 adults, $15 children 3–12. June 19–Sept 15 daily 9am–5:30pm.*

Day 4
★★ kids **Kootenay National Park.** Less visited, and wonderfully expansive, Kootenay is an off-the-beaten-path destination that makes a great day trip from Banff. This park is particularly friendly to fami-lies, with lots of kids in strollers and some great picnic spots. **START: Town of Banff.**

Drive the Trans-Canada Hwy. 1 west to Castle Junction and take Hwy. 93 south. Length: 132km (82 miles) each way.

Travel Tip

Driving Hwy. 93 at dusk is prime wildlife-viewing time, so keep an eye out and drive safely.

You can find hundreds of species of wildflowers while hiking at Sunshine Meadows.

1 ★ **kids** **Fireweed Trail.** A 20-minute loop explains why natural forest fires are healthy and good for the environment. As you continue on through Kootenay, you may be driving through a number of fire sites, so getting the lowdown here will help you understand and appreciate the burned landscapes. ⏱ *15 min. 95km (59 miles) from Radium, on the Alberta–British Columbia (and Banff–Kootenay) border.*

Continue southwest on Hwy. 93.

2 ★★ **Stanley Glacier.** One of my favorite shorter hikes in the Rockies, this trail takes you from fire (a lightning-provoked burn from 1968) to ice (the Stanley Glacier) in just 2.5km (1.5 miles). Most of the 395 meters (1,296 ft.) to be climbed are at the beginning, leaving you time to amble amidst a hanging valley with awesome views. Great for families. ⏱ *3 hr. Trail head is 3.2km (2 miles) west of the Alberta–British Columbia (and Banff–Kootenay national parks) border on south side of highway.*

3 **Marble Canyon.** A narrow trail of limestone carved by two retreating glaciers, this is a great spot on a hot day. It's cool and shady. Kids will find this short hike intriguing, but keep a sharp eye on them because the trail can get very slippery. ⏱ *30 min. 89km (55 miles) from Radium, 7km (4⅓ miles) from Alberta–British Columbia (and Banff–Kootenay national parks) border on north side of highway.*

4 ★ **Paint Pots.** Natives came together at these remote cold springs to gather ocher, an iron-based mineral that was baked, crushed, mixed with grease, and used as a paint for tepees, pictographs, and personal adornment. There's an excellent wheelchair- and stroller-friendly 30-minute interpretive trail. ⏱ *40 min. 85km (53 miles) from Radium, 10km (6¼ miles) from Alberta–British Columbia (and Banff–Kootenay national parks) border on north side of highway.*

5 ★★ **Radium Hot Springs Pool.** Nestled in a canyon rich with oxide, these "sacred mountain waters" are surrounded by an orange-sunset vibe. The pools are more spacious than those in Banff, and there are often bighorn sheep mulling about. ⏱ *2 hr. See p 114.*

6 **Sinclair Canyon.** With this stunning farewell, Kootenay closes with a bang just shy of the village of Radium Hot Springs. Your car barely sneaks through iron-rich cliffs that are part of the Redwall Fault and form a dramatic entrance to the Columbia Valley. There's a small roadside pull-off just west of the canyon where you can get out of the car to walk through the giant walls and take photos, which will be especially gorgeous at sunset. Watch for bighorn sheep on the roadside. ⏱ *10 min. 1.5km (1 mile) from Radium and 131km (81 miles) from Alberta–British Columbia (and*

Natives once used the colorful minerals from these cold springs to make paints.

The soothing mineral waters of the Radium Hot Springs Pool.

Banff–Kootenay national parks) border in the middle of the highway.

Day 5

Travel from Banff to Lake Louise, following Day 3 of "Banff in 1 Week," p 19.

Day 6

Hiking Paradise Valley. Rewarding and challenging, this hike starts in Paradise Valley, just south of Lake Louise. You'll take in a long list of highlights, like the "Giant's Staircase," Lake Annette, and gorgeous views of Mt. Temple. It's a 22km (13.6-mile) hike that will take you all day. *See p 145. Trail head: Paradise Valley parking lot 2.5km (1½ miles) south from Lake Louise Rd.*

Day 7

Visit Yoho National Park as described in Day 6 of "Best of Banff in 1 Week," p 19.

Day 8

Camping at Lake O'Hara. Just the mention of Yoho National Park's Lake O'Hara makes die-hard hikers get misty in the eyes. It's also a

great first-camping outing, since you access the backcountry campground via a Parks Canada–run bus—meaning you don't have to carry a heavy load and you can camp in comfort. The bus departs daily from a parking lot just off the Trans-Canada Highway at 8:30am, 10:30am, 3:30pm, and 5:30pm, and you must have a reservation. Once you've set up your tent and settled in, hike around the namesake lake for orientation, and then head over past Schäffer Lake to beautiful Lake McArthur, a great 2- to 3-hour hike. *See p 108.*

Day 9

Hiking at Lake O'Hara. Few places in the world can rival the stunning scenery, historic trail system, varied landscape, and special charm of this tiny area tucked beneath the Continental Divide. Spend your day on the Lake O'Hara Alpine Circuit, one of the best hikes in the entire world. It'll lead you past such glorious sites as the Opabin Plateau, the Yukness Ledges, and Lake Oesa. After taking the bus from just outside the Relais Day Shelter back to the parking lot (the last bus

Sinclair Canyon marks the striking exit out of Kootenay.

A hiker crosses a bridge in Paradise Valley.

of the day leaves at 6:30pm), head back to Lake Louise. *See p 108.*

Day 10

Today follows Day 3 of "Banff In Three Days" (p 16), but continues past the Icefields Centre and on to the Town of Jasper. Follow Hwy. 93, the Icefields Parkway, north 105km (65 miles) to Jasper Townsite. You should have time to squeeze in the outstanding hike to **Wilcox Pass** (p 148) as well, for a jaw-dropping lookout of the Columbia Icefield. See p 46.

Day 11

Tour of Jasper Townsite and Area. Located in an expansive valley on the west bank of the Athabasca River, Jasper's off-season population hovers around 5,000, but blossoms to more than 20,000 in the summer, when university students from across Canada head here for summer jobs and to mingle with the thousands of travelers passing through, turning the somewhat sleepy mountain town into a vibrant destination. The town itself is quite large, but most visitors will stick to the two main drags, Connaught Drive and Patricia Street. That's where you'll find the good restaurants, shops, and outfitters. **START: Jasper Information Centre. Length: 72km (45 miles).**

❶ ★ Jasper National Park Information Centre. Stop here

The Jasper National Park's Information Centre is a great place to get advice and pick up maps and permits.

to pick up permits, maps, and brochures, and to have the friendly staff help you make the most of your day. ⏲ *20 min. 500 Connaught Dr.* ☎ *780/852-6176.*

Head west across Connaught Drive (also known as Hwy. 93), continuing through the lights at the junction with Hwy. 16. Take the first right on Whistlers Road, continuing uphill until you reach:

② ★ **Jasper Tramway.** Your quickest and easiest way to the high alpine terrain, this 7-minute gondola ride takes you up 973m (3,192 ft.), just short of the summit of Whistlers Mountain. From the top, the views of the Athabasca and Miette valleys are stunning. There's a well marked, though quite steep, 45-minute self-guided trail to the summit of the mountain. Watch for hoary marmots and white-tailed ptarmigan. Lineups can be intense, so try to head there in the morning. ⏲ *90 min. 3km (1¾ miles) south of Jasper on Hwy. 93, turn left/west on the Whistler Mountain Rd. for another 4km (2½ miles).* ☎ *866/850-8726 and 780/852-3093. Adults $31, kids 5–14 $16. April 7– May 18 daily 10am–5pm; May 19– June 22 daily 9:30am–6:30pm; June 23–Aug 29 daily 9am–8pm; Aug 30– Oct 8 daily 10am–5pm.*

Return to Hwy. 93 and head south 21km (13 miles) to the junction with Hwy. 93A, which heads north. Just past the turnoff is:

③ **Athabasca Falls.** Known more for its force than its height, this is one of the most impressive waterfalls in the Rockies, where the Athabasca River (the same one born at the Columbia Icefield and the most important river in Jasper National Park) thunders over a layer of hard quartzite and through a narrow limestone gorge. ⏲ *20 min. 25km (15 miles) south of Jasper.*

Continue north on the scenic Hwy. 93A, 18km (11 miles) to the Cavell Road, a narrow and winding mountain road that requires much attention from drivers. At 15km (9½ miles), you'll arrive at the parking lot beneath:

④ ★★ **Mt. Edith Cavell.** This is the highest, and arguably the most scenic mountain in all of Jasper, named for a World War I British nurse. The Angel Glacier saddles the northeastern slope and sends a tongue of ice off the cliff side into a milky blue lake. The Path of the Glacier Trail takes you over boulders, shrubbery, pebbles, and sand through a landscape that, less than a century ago, was covered by a glacier. ⏲ *45 min. Follow Hwy. 93A to the Cavell Rd. Continue another 12km (7½ miles) to the parking lot.*

Take the Cavell Road back to Hwy. 93A. Turn left and continue 5.2km (3¼ miles) to the junction with Hwy. 93. Turn left and drive north into the Town of Jasper. Park your car next to the Heritage Railway Station. Cross Connaught Drive and walk up Miette Avenue to Patricia Street.

⑤ ★ **Coco's Café.** Where laidback locals come to grab lunch, this busy little joint on Patricia Street has yummy wraps, curries, and soups that make superb lunches. There are also great cappuccinos, lattes, and espresso. The cafe is small and can be cramped; expect to literally rub elbows with your neighbors. *608 Patricia St.* ☎ *780/852-4550. $.*

⑥ ★ **Patricia Street.** Now that you've seen the major highlights south and west of town, spend the afternoon strolling the charming shops of Jasper's main streets. Focus on Patricia Street between Hazel Avenue and Cedar Street, and

Mt. Edith Cavell, Jasper's tallest mountain.

then loop back along Connaught Drive. Slow down, enjoy the expansive views, and pick up a souvenir or two. **Counter Clockwise Emporium** (616 Patricia St.; ☎ 780/852-3152) has everything from books and jewelry to soaps and furniture.

Walking back towards your car, cross Connaught Drive at Miette Avenue and pop into the:

❼ Heritage Railway Station. You can still picture Victorian ladies with their parasols and elaborate dresses mixing with rough 'n' tumble gold diggers at this old frontier outpost, now housing the park administration offices as well as a train station. Trains heading east and west across Canada, including the VIA Rail passenger trains, stop here daily. It's still a hub. ⏱ *10 min. On Connaught Dr. across from Whistler's Hotel.*

❽ Old Fort Point. Jutting out into the Athabasca River, the point offers great views that take in Jasper Townsite, Lac Beauvert, and the Fairmont Jasper Park Lodge. From here you can also catch sight of Mt. Kerkeslin and Mt. Hardisty to the southeast, and the snowy triangle of Mt. Edith Cavell, shining above all others, to the south. It's a 2-hour hike atop a glacier-carved knoll to complete the loop via the lookout. Hike counter-clockwise for a gentler climb. ⏱ *2 hr. To access Old Fort Point, drive 5 min. south of Jasper Townsite via Hwy. 93A and Old Fort Point Rd. See p 105.*

Day 12

The Maligne Valley is a classic glacier-carved hanging valley and a natural wonderland. Have your camera ready—it's also a prime wildlife-viewing spot. Watch for moose, bighorn sheep, bears, and caribou! **START: Jasper Information Centre. Trip Length: 97km (60 miles) return.**

Take Connaught Drive east out of town until it joins with Hwy. 16, the Yellowhead Highway. Continue 4km (2½ miles) east to the bridge over the Athabasca River. Turn right. This is the beginning of the Maligne Valley Road.

❶ ★★ Maligne Canyon. A waterfall in slow motion, this limestone canyon is at the lip of the Maligne Valley as it meets the much lower Athabasca Valley. There is a lovely series of bridges and walkways that bring you close up to the largest underground drainage system known in Canada. At some points it's only 2m (6.5 ft.) across and 50m (164 ft.) deep! Starting at the upper bridge allows you to see the main highlights. Keep right at all intersections of the self-guided interpretive trail, and then loop back up. ⏱ *30 min. At km 7 (mile 4⅓) on Maligne Valley Rd.*

Continue south on the Maligne Valley Road until you reach:

❷ Medicine Lake. This could be called Mystery Lake—with no visible drainage, this lake seems to evaporate into nothing. The early Natives believed this mysterious lake had healing powers, hence the name. 🕐 *10 min. At km 21 (mile 13) on the Maligne Valley Rd.*

Continue south on the Maligne Valley Road until you reach:

❸ kids ★★ Maligne Lake Cruise Spirit Island. A 90-minute cruise on a glass-bottomed boat to a tiny, precious island, dotted with a handful of skinny pines and tucked in a placid corner of this glorious lake (the largest lake in Jasper National Park and the second largest glacial lake in the world) is a great outing for families. The island itself is shrouded in mystery and legends, which the guides explain en route. From the deck, watch for eagles, mountain goats, and even the odd avalanche, if it's the right time of year. 🕐 *90 min. At km 45 (mile 28) on the Maligne Valley Rd. Adults $55, kids 5–14 $27.50. Daily departures hourly from boat docks: thaw date—June 4 10am–3pm; June 5–June 30 and Sept 1–Oct 4 10am–4pm; July 1–Aug 31 10am–5pm.*

Return north on the Maligne Valley Road. Just before the Athabasca River bridge, turn left on Old Lodge Road. You'll pass Lakes Annette and Edith before arriving at:

❹ ★★ Fairmont Jasper Park Lodge. The largest commercial property in the Canadian Rocky Mountain National Parks, this classic wilderness lodge attracts tourists and dignitaries from around the world. Hike the hour-long walk around Lac Beauvert, rent a canoe for a paddle on the lake, enjoy a meal at one of the hotel's six restaurants, or play a round on the award-winning golf course. 🕐 *60 min. 3.2km (2 miles) west of Maligne Valley Rd. on Old Lodge Rd.* 📞 *780/852-3301.*

❺ Tea at the "JPL." More cozy and casual than its sister hotels (the Banff Springs and the Chateau Lake Louise), tea here is likewise comfortable and delectable, with elegant sandwiches and pastries to accompany more than a dozen teas. Served daily between 2 and 4:30pm in the Emerald Lounge, overlooking Lac Beauvert, Mt. Edith Cavell, and the Whistler's Mountain. *Old Lodge Rd.* 📞 *780/852-3301. $$.*

Jasper's Heritage Railway Station transports visitors back in time.

You'll find spectacular views at the award-winning golf course at Jasper Park Lodge.

Day 13

kids Rafting on Athabasca River. Choose between a family-friendly scenic float trip down the Athabasca River, or Class III on the Sunwapta River. (Sunwapta is a Stoney Indian word meaning "turbulent river.") The big rapid is known as "the Whopper." *Jasper Raft Tours departs for the river daily at 12:30pm from the Jasper Railway Station. $64 adults, $25 youth 15–17, $20 kids 5–14, $5 kids 4 and under. 611 Patricia St.* ☎ *780/852-2665. www.jasperrafttours.com.*

If rafting's not up your alley, book a round at the Fairmont Jasper Park Lodge's 18-hole course. *(4km/2½ miles east of Jasper Town-site on Hwy. 16, then south on Maligne Lake Rd. and a quick left/ west after the bridge, follow 3.2km/*

2 miles to end. Tee times daily 7am– 6pm. ☎ *780/852-6090. www. fairmont.com/jasper. Green fees $120–$180).*

Day 14

Grab breakfast at Bear's Paw (p 127), 610 Connaught Dr.; the original is still at 4 Cedar Ave.; ☎ 780/852-3233. If you are heading back to Banff, drive south along the Icefields Parkway, retracing your steps. It's 287km (178 miles) or 3½ hours if you don't stop, but you'll likely discover the drive equally intriguing and beautiful in a southerly direction. Plan to stop for some photographing and leg-stretching. If you are heading to Edmonton, which is 370km (230 miles) and about 4 hours east, plan to stop for a soak at the Miette Hot Springs en route. See p 102. ●

Banff **for Photographers**

△	Campground
⛽	Gasoline
✚	Hospital/First Aid
ⓘ	Information

DAY 1

1 Lake Minnewanka
2 Vermillion Lakes
3 Mt. Norquay Road
4 Surprise Corner
5 Eddie Burger and Bar
6 Cascade Gardens
7 Castle Mountain
8 Kootenay Parkway

DAY 2

9 Lake Louise
10 Moraine Lake
☕ Trailhead Café
12 Herbert Lake
13 Peyto Lake

Previous page: Big-horn sheep are a common sight in Banff National Park.

Banff National Park is one of the most photographed places in the entire world. Even amateur shutterbugs will be delighted here, where each turn brings another postcard-worthy view. Focusing in on the ultimate photo ops involves timing, patience, and flexibility. But if you get up early and follow these stops, you'll surely gather a series of award-winners. START: **Town of Banff.**

Day 1

Head out of Banff on Banff Avenue, going northeast towards Cascade Mountain. Cross under the Trans-Canada Hwy. 1 and continue on:

❶ Minnewanka Road. The easiest place for morning wildlife sightings is this drive just northeast of Banff. Watch for bighorn sheep near Two Jack Lake. A photo of Lake Minnewanka in a storm can be extremely dramatic.

Continue across the Trans-Canada Highway to the second Banff exit. Turn right (west) on Vermillion Lakes Road and continue to where the road ends.

❷ Mt. Rundle from Vermillion Lakes. The stillness of the morning on these shallow lakes brings birdlife and moose. Late afternoon often offers alpine glow on the ridges of Rundle, that unforgettable peak that may be the most famous in all of Banff. In the summer you can paddle into the middle of the lake for an undisturbed shot—or

skate out on the frozen lakes in the winter for an icy masterpiece.

Take a left at Mt. Norquay Road.

❸ Mt. Norquay Road. For a great shot that takes in all of the Town of Banff, as well as its scenic surroundings, head up the switchbacks of the Mt. Norquay Road to the turnoff.

Drive back into Banff along Mt. Norquay Road, which turns into Gopher Street and then becomes Lynx Street. Turn left at Buffalo Street and continue past Banff Avenue. After the housing ends, the forest thickens. At the next main switchback, park and get out of the car.

❹ Surprise Corner. At an elbow bend on the edge of Tunnel Mountain, this is the classic viewpoint for admiring the Fairmont Banff Springs Hotel in all its glory. Sulphur Mountain forms the backdrop, and the majestic Bow Falls rumble beneath. Head up toward the Banff Centre on Buffalo Street, and keep an eye out for fellow photographers crossing the street!

Mt. Rundle may be the most famous peak in Banff.

Cascade Gardens at Canada Place with Cascade Mountain on the horizon.

Head back into town on Buffalo Street and turn left at Banff Avenue.

5 Lunch at Eddie Burger and Bar. You're hungry and on a tight schedule. For a quick, hearty lunch, you can't beat the home-made burgers at this joint on Caribou. *137C Banff Ave. (on Caribou St.). ☎ 403/762-2230. $$. See p 72.*

Fallow Banff Avenue over the Bow River Bridge. Take a left at the end of the bridge and a quick right into the parking lot.

6 Cascade Gardens. At the far end of Banff Avenue, these land-scaped gardens provide a great per-spective on the hustle and bustle, not to mention the stunning back-ground, of Banff's main drag. Cas-cade Mountain rises like a pyramid in the distance. Walk from the park-ing lot to a lookout across the Bow River Bridge. The gardens are open all day June through September and are free to visit.

Drive back out of town, take the Mt. Norquay Road, and then turn left (west) at the Trans-Canada Hwy. 1. The views begin from about 10km (6¼ miles) west of Banff.

7 Castle Mountain. There are many wonderful angles for capturing the many fine details of this beast of a mountain, between Banff and Lake Louise. With the Bow River in your foreground, there'll be many colors. Catch the late afternoon light from the west side of the Vermillion Pass, towards the British Columbia border from Castle Junction.

Turn west on Hwy. 93 toward Radium Hot Springs.

8 The Kootenay Parkway. Hwy. 93 runs from Castle Junction to Radium Hot Springs in British Colum-bia, through Kootenay National Park. This is prime wildlife-viewing terri-tory, particularly at dusk. White-tailed deer, bear, moose, coyotes, bighorn sheep, and mountain goats can all be seen. Key spots are at Moose Mead-ows picnic area, the ink spots near Hector Gorge, and the stretch between Crooks Meadows and Koo-tenay Crossing.

Day 2
From the Town of Banff, head west on the Trans-Canada Hwy. 1, 58km (36 miles) to Lake Louise. Turn off the highway and head up Lake Louise Road to the famous lake.

1 Lake Louise. There's no wonder it's the most photographed lake in Canada. Beautifully framed by tall peaks, with a shimmering surface and a glacier at the back, come here mid-morning for the best light. In winter, that means between 10am and noon. In summer, aim for an 8:30am start for a shot including the boat docks.

Head down 2.5km (1½ miles) on Lake Louise Road, turning right on the Moraine Lake Road and following it for 13km (8 miles).

2 Moraine Lake. I've seen the image of this pristine lake on every-thing from the former $10 bill to a beer advertisement. The Valley of the

Photographing Wildlife

Depending on the time of year and your luck, you'll see a wide range of wildlife while roaming Banff National Park with your camera. June is ideal for black bears; late fall is good for bull elks and moose. It's important, though, to respect park rules and always maintain a safe viewing distance from the animals. Usually, this means at least 30m (98 ft.), but for big animals like moose and bear, keep at least 100m (328 ft.) away.

Ten Peaks in the background oozes with drama. Come before noon.

Retrace your route and turn right on Lake Louise Road, returning to Lake Louise village.

3 Trailhead Café. Pick up lunch to go at this busy little cafe in Samson Mall. Grab a fresh wrap—there are more than a dozen to choose from, but I love the tropical wrap with chicken and mango salsa, or the donair wraps with lamb. They pack up nice and clean for a picnic later on. *In Samson Mall.* ☎ 403/522-2006. $.

Head west on the Trans-Canada Highway and then north on the Icefields Parkway towards Jasper

to 2.5km (1½ miles) north of the Icefields Parkway gate.

4 Herbert Lake. Because this lake is both small and sheltered by the tall peaks around it, it provides glass-like reflection in the morning, with the sun shining on the Bow Range in front, as well as Mt. Bosworth to the north or Mt. Temple and the peaks of Lake Louise to the south.

Continue north on the Icefields Parkway another 39km (24 miles).

5 Peyto Lake. With a blue deeper than the waters of the Caribbean, and steep edges of mountainside all around, Peyto Lake is a must-stop on the Icefields Parkway. In July and August, wildflowers are blooming. It's well worth the short stroll to the lookout.

Photographers head to Lake Louise in the morning to capture a breathtaking view.

Banff **with Kids**

DAY 1

1. Sulphur Mountain Gondola
2. Banff Park Museum
3. Sushi Train!
4. Biking on the Sundance Trail or Golf Course Loop
5. Fairmont Banff Springs Hotel
6. Grizzly House
7. Evening Interpretive Theater

DAY 2

8. Hiking to Boom Lake

DAY 3

9. Lake Louise Sightseeing Gondola
10. Bill Peyto's Café
11. Columbia Glacier Icefield Experience

Map labels:

0 — 10 mi
0 — 10 km

To Jasper National Park

Park Gate
Saskatchewan Crossing

LYELL ICEFIELD
Siffleur Wilderness

FRESHFIELD ICEFIELD

BRITISH COLUMBIA

WAPTA ICEFIELD

YOHO NATIONAL PARK
Field
Kicking Horse Pass

Icefields Parkway

ALBERTA

BANFF NATIONAL PARK
Red Deer River
Bow River

Lake Louise Village
Temple Mtn.
Castle Junction
Castle Mtn.
Cascade Mtn.
Johnston Canyon
Banff
Area of inset

KOOTENAY NATIONAL PARK
Vermillion River

Mt. Assiniboine Provincial Park

Radium Hot Springs
Park Gate

Legend:
△ Campground
⛽ Gasoline
ⓘ Information
P Parking
■ Point of Interest

Inset (Edmonton area):
Edmonton
ALBERTA
Jasper
BRITISH COLUMBIA
Lake Louise
Golden
Calgary
Banff
Area of map
CANADA
UNITED STATES

Banff inset:
Wolf
Caribou
Lynx
Bear
Otter
Banff Av.
Glen Av.
Spray Av.
Tunnel Mountain Dr.
St.-Julien Rd.
Bow River
Spray River
Mountain Av.
Banff

Families flock to Banff for adventure, nature, and quality time surrounded by inspiring fresh air. Lifelong mountain lovers are born here every day—just ask the locals, most of whom first fell for these peaks on a family vacation. The keys to keeping kids engaged include getting out of the car a lot, following your nose with a sense of adventure and discovery, and keeping track of all that you see and learn. START: **Your hotel in Banff.**

Day 1

Drive south on Banff Avenue, over the Bow River Bridge. Turn left and then right quickly on to Mountain Road. Follow until it ends at:

❶ Sulphur Mountain Gondola. This may be your child's first summit, and the thrill won't soon be forgotten. After the 8-minute gondola ride drops you on top of the world, hike the 700 steps, across a secure boardwalk, to the top of Samson's Peak. ⏱ *90 min. See p 13.*

Head back down Mountain Avenue, turning left onto Spray Road and right over the Bow River Bridge. Take a quick left onto Buffalo Street, and then turn left into the parking lots between Central Park and:

❷ Banff Park Museum National Historic Site. Kids will like the discovery room inside this natural history museum, which is

Thousands of wildlife species are on display at the Banff Park Museum.

inside a log building built in 1903. With more than 5,000 species of birds, insects, and wildlife on display, it's a one-stop shop for learning about the Rockies. Great on a rainy day. ⏱ *45 min. See p 52.*

You can leave your car parked next to the museum. Walk up Banff Avenue, turning right at Caribou Street. Half a block later, on your left-hand side is:

❸ Sushi Train! Family-friendly restaurants are a dime a dozen in Banff. But adventurous kids will love to choose pieces of sushi off a model train carrying the food around the counter at the tiny Sushi House Restaurant. Each dish is priced according to the color of the plate—and just ask the sushi master inside the tracks if there's something special you'd like. The food is fresh and healthy, and the atmosphere is convivial and fun. *304 Caribou St.* ☎ *403/762-4353. $.*

Walk to the west end of Caribou Street, turning left on Bear Street to the shop for:

❹ Biking. Kids love to try new things. Rent a bike in Banff and head up the Sundance Trail towards Sundance Canyon. The 3.7km (2.3-mile) trail has little elevation gain and is paved the entire way. Another option good for families is the 15km (9.3-mile) Golf Course Loop. It's peaceful and pretty. *Adventures Unlimited (211 Bear St.;* ☎ *403/762-4554) rents kids' bikes, trailers, and strollers.*

At Sushi Train!, diners select dishes that are delivered via a model railroad.

After dropping off your bikes, return to your car. Drive back over the Bow River Bridge, taking a left onto Spray Road. Follow it until it ends at:

⑤ The "Castle in the Rockies." Little girls will love to put on a party dress and explore inside the utterly distinctive Fairmont Banff Springs Hotel. Before you settle in for an English-style tea, roam medieval corridors and find your way down mysterious corners. ⏱ *90 min. Tea in the Rundle Lounge $38 adults, $18 children 6–12. 405 Spray Ave.* ☎ *403/762-6860.*

From Banff Avenue, turn east or right on Wolf Street, and then northeast or left on Tunnel Mountain Road. Drive 4km (2½ miles) to the entrance to Tunnel Mountain Campground:

Enjoying a family-friendly bike route.

⑥ Grizzly House. Mixing Gilligan's island with Heidi's alpine shack, there is loads of personality here. It's noisy and raucous, great for energetic families. The specialties are cheese or beef fondues, but the most exotic version has you hot-dipping shark, alligator, rattlesnake, ostrich, and frogs' legs. *207 Banff Ave.* ☎ *403/762-4055. $$.*

⑦ Evening Interpretive Theater. Nature interpreters from Banff National Park offer a variety of evening activities at the Tunnel Mountain Theatre, inside the Tunnel Mountain Campground. Throughout the summer, there are daily programs at 7:30pm, ranging from a historical rendition of Banff's legendary characters to stories of adventure in the peaks. They're fun, participatory, and a great learning experience. Best of all, they're free! ⏱ *45 min. Contact Parks Canada for updated schedules at* ☎ *403/762-1550.*

Day 2
Grab a picnic lunch, bear spray, some water, sunscreen, and rain gear, and hit the trails. Drive west from Banff on the Trans-Canada Hwy. 1, 28km (17 miles) to Castle Junction. Turn west onto Hwy. 93A S.

Hiking to Boom Lake. Scores of life-long hikers have had their first thrills on the trail here in Banff. There are many kid-friendly hikes to choose from. I suggest the relatively gentle climb to Boom Lake, which is surrounded by a massive limestone wall along the Continental Divide. The trail has a real sense of discovery to it. Bring a picnic—it's a 10km (6.2-mile) return trip that will take you 4 hours or so. *Trail head is off Hwy. 93 S., 7km (4 miles) west of Castle Junction.*

Day 3

Head out of Banff, west on the Trans-Canada Hwy. 1 58km (36 miles) to the turnoff for Lake Louise. Turn right, heading up the hill to:

❶ Lake Louise Sightseeing Gondola. Kids are both scared and intrigued by grizzly bears, and this is a superb place to learn more about the often-misunderstood beast that rules the Banff backcountry. Interpretive guides explain how the "grizz" makes its home. ⏱ *2 hr. See p 63.*

Drive down the hill, over the Trans-Canada Hwy. 1. At the main intersection, turn right on Village Road right past Samson Mall. Past the red-roofed Post Hotel, take a left into the entrance for:

❷ Bill Peyto's Café. Located inside the Lake Louise Hostel and Alpine Centre, the food is healthy, creative, and priced for most budgets. The timber-framed room with stone fireplace makes for a relaxed, friendly atmosphere. Service is fast. Try the bison burgers, chicken pesto burger, or macaroni and cheese. There's also a kids' menu. *In the Lake Louise Hostel and Alpine Centre. 203 Village Rd.* ☎ *403/522-2200. $.*

Exit Lake Louise, turning west or left onto the Trans-Canada Hwy. 1. Turn north on Hwy. 93, the Icefields Parkway, continuing for 130km (81 miles) until you reach:

❸ The Columbia Glacier Icefield Experience. Hop on a giant tractor-like bus called a "snocoach" with sky-high wheels, drive onto a frozen tongue of ice, and then hike out on the ice—not your average day in the park. Tours leave every 15 minutes or so. It's best to visit the icefield in the mornings or late afternoon to avoid the throngs of tourists arriving by bus from the towns of Banff and Jasper. ⏱ *Tour lasts 90 min. See p 17.*

This "snocoach" takes adventurous tourists into the icefield.

Banff **in Wintertime**

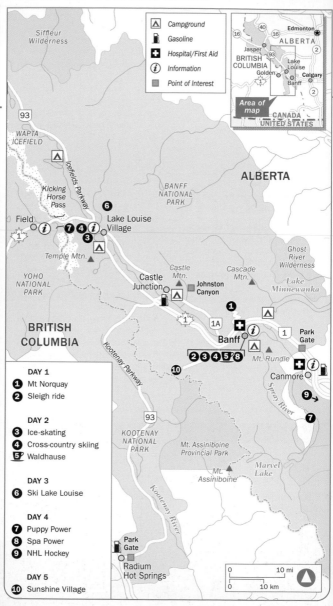

LEGEND

- 🅰 Campground
- ⛽ Gasoline
- ➕ Hospital/First Aid
- ⓘ Information
- ◼ Point of Interest

DAY 1
1. Mt Norquay
2. Sleigh ride

DAY 2
3. Ice-skating
4. Cross-country skiing
5. Waldhause

DAY 3
6. Ski Lake Louise

DAY 4
7. Puppy Power
8. Spa Power
9. NHL Hockey

DAY 5
10. Sunshine Village

| 0 | 10 mi |
| 0 | 10 km |

Banff becomes a winter wonderland from late November through early April. Famous for its crisp blue skies, winter in the Canadian Rockies is just as beautiful as summer. In fact, many people swear that winter is an even better time to visit. For those not hindered by the cold, skiing in Banff is a one-of-a-kind experience. And don't forget all those snowmen and women waiting to be built and evening strolls waiting to be taken under star-studded skies, often active with the stunning *aurora borealis* ("northern lights").

Day 1

① Alpine Skiing at Mt. Norquay. A week is just barely enough to sample the best the area has to offer. Together, the three ski resorts in Banff—Mt. Norquay, Sunshine Village, and Ski Louise—make this one of the great ski destinations in North America. I recommend visiting them each for at least a day. For Day 6, you could return to whichever you liked best (and that's an endless debate that rages on in Banff and will give you plenty to chat to folks about on the chairlift!). The SkiBig 3 partnership sells a package to all three (☎ 877/754-7080 or 403/762-4561; www.skibig3.com). **Mt. Norquay** is a locals' favorite because it's intimate and less than 15 minutes from Banff Avenue. There's plenty of intermediate runs there to stretch your legs on. Economical ski-by-the-hour deals are good for days when you want to take it easy. ☎ *403/762-4421. www.banff norquay.com. See p 157.*

Evening 1

② Sleigh Ride. For a romantic winter evening, snuggle up under a cozy blanket with someone special, join a cowboy, and head out for a one-horse open-sleigh ride with Holiday on Horseback. *132 Banff Ave.* ☎ *403/762-4551. $29 adults, $25 children 4–12.*

Day 2

① Ice-Skating. There are a number of places where you can skate outdoors under the winter sky. It's an exhilarating activity that's popular with families. Try the Vermillion Lakes, just outside the Town of

Skating on Vermillion Lakes.

Cross-country skiing just before sunset.

Louise, which starts just in front of the Chateau Lake Louise. See p 158 for ski-rental information.

3 On a crisp winter night, your cheeks aglow from a day in the mountains, what could be more divine than a steaming pot of Alpine-inspired fondue? The best fondue in Banff is at the **Waldhaus,** a Bavarian-style cottage in the woods beneath the Fairmont Banff Springs Hotel. *405 Spray Ave.* ☎ *403/762-6860. $$$. See p 79.*

Day 3
Ski Lake Louise. For jaw-dropping views, coupled with an incredibly varied terrain, head to this legendary ski resort across the valley from the infamous lake. Be sure to drop by cozy Temple Lodge for lunch. ☎ *800/258-7669 or 403/522-3555. www.skilouise.com. See p 157.*

Day 4
1 Puppy Power. It's one of the oldest forms of transportation in the world. Dog-sledding is offered just

Dog-sledding outside of the Town of Banff.

Banff, in the early winter before the snow starts to pile up. Take Mt. Norquay Road out of town, turning left on Vermillion Lakes Drive just before the Trans-Canada Hwy. 1. You can rent skates in Banff at **Snowtips** *(225 Bear St.; ☎ 403/762-8177; from $14/day).* At the Fairmont Chateau Lake Louise, there is an outdoor rink on the lake with a spectacular ice castle built right on top. It's a very scenic and romantic place to skate. *At the top of Lake Louise Dr. Rent skates at Chateau Mountain Sports inside the hotel. ☎ 403/522-3837; from $10 for 2 hr. or $14/day.*

2 Cross-Country Skiing. A wonderful way to explore the park in winter, cross-country (or "Nordic") skiing promises great exercise, views, and solitude, if you're seeking it. There are more than 80km (50 miles) of managed trails in Banff National Park, many of them within a half-hour drive of Banff Townsite. The cross-country ski season runs from December to March. Try the Spray River Loop, which departs from the parking lot at Bow Falls, and the Shoreline Trail at Lake

You Are in Avalanche Country

The Canadian Rockies is avalanche country. An extremely powerful wave of snow and ice that cracks off a mountain slope, an avalanche can destroy everything in its path. It's extremely challenging to predict when an avalanche might occur, and even more challenging to escape if you are caught in one. Drivers should avoid stopping in areas where Parks Canada has posted an AVALANCHE ZONE sign. Parks Canada updates avalanche forecasts regularly throughout the winter. In Banff, call ☎ 403/762-1460.

outside Banff in Kananaskis Country. Drive the dogs or just ride along as you mush your way across a frozen lake. *Book through Snowy Owl Tours.* ☎ *403/678-4369. www.snowyowl tours.com. 104–602 Bow Valley Trail, Canmore. $149–$385 per person.*

❷ Spa Power. Work off all those kinks with a visit to the truly outstanding, private, and decadent **Willowstream Spa** at the Fairmont Banff Hot Springs. After soaking in the mineral pools, indulge in a mountain stone massage or an après-ski massage. *405 Spray Ave.* ☎ *800/404-1772 or 403/762-2211. From $189 for 60 min.*

Evening 3 or 4
❸ NHL Hockey. Hockey is a fast-paced game, and you'll catch some of the world's best ice hockey players in action at the Calgary Saddledome, cheering on the NHL's Calgary Flames. Pure Canadiana! *Book through Banff Adventures Unlimited (*☎ *403/762-4554; www. banffadventures.com), which has shuttles from Banff for all Flames home games.*

Day 5
Sunshine Village. Tucked along the Continental Divide, beautiful Sunshine Village generally has the

best snow, lots of good intermediate runs, and the notoriously extreme Delirium Dive, for experts only. Sunshine also has the best terrain park in the area and magnificent views of Mt. Assiniboine. ☎ *800/661-1676 or 403/762-6500. www.skibanff.com. See p 157.*

Skiing through fresh powder at Sunshine Village.

Glaciers & Wildlife

GLACIERS

1 Mt. Temple
2 Mt. Victoria
3 Bath Glacier
4 Crowfoot Glacier
5 Bow Glacier
6 Snowbird Glacier
7 Saskatchewan Glacier
8 Columbia Icefield
9 Athabasca Glacier
10 Snow Dome

WILDLIFE

11 Urban Elk in Town of Banff
12 Minnwanka Loop
13 Muleshoe
14 Bourgeau Wildlife Overpass
15 Helen Lake
16 Bow Summit
17 Waterfowl Lakes
18 Mt. Coleman

Studying the cycles of nature in the incredible mountain wilderness of the Canadian Rockies is enlightening, astounding, and inspiring. There are more than 1,000 glaciers in Banff, and all of them are retreating. Scientists say the glaciers of Banff lost 25% of their mass during the 20th century. Most can't be seen from the convenience of the major highways. There is, however, an easy-to-access and varied selection you can spot from the roadside, ranging from almost-hidden glaciers like the Snowbird to the most famous glacier in North America, the Athabasca. **START: Lake Louise.**

Travel Tip

Most of these glaciers are northeast facing, so the light will be better for seeing them in the first half of the day.

Glaciers in Banff National Park

❶ Mt. Temple. This may be my favorite peak in Banff. With a giant pyramid-like shape and a beautiful glacier below its summit, Mt. Temple dominates the horizon south of Lake Louise. *6km (3¾ miles) east of Lake Louise on Trans-Canada Hwy. 1.*

❷ Mt. Victoria. One of the most photographed mountains in the world, this wide peak provides the scenic backdrop to Lake Louise. Always snow covered, it's best appreciated from the 5.3km (3.3-mile) hike to the Plain of the Six Glaciers, where the Aberdeen, Upper Lefroy, Lower Lefroy, Upper Victoria, Lower Victoria, and Pope's glaciers (as seen left to

right or southeast to southwest) are all visible. It's a 4-hour round-trip that departs from the shore of Lake Louise just past the Fairmont Chateau Lake Louise, heading to the right around the lake. *See p 145.*

❸ Bath Glacier. Part of the mighty Waputik Icefield, the Bath Glacier hugs the midridge of Mt. Daly. It can be seen at Mt. Hector, just north of Lake Louise. *17km (11 miles) north of Lake Louise on Hwy. 93.*

❹ Crowfoot Glacier. Years ago, there were three toe-like extensions of this glacier clinging to the side of a cliff. The lowest "toe" has retreated completely, leaving a rare two-toed crow. *32km (20 miles) north of Lake Louise on Hwy. 93.*

❺ Bow Glacier. Visible at the back of the valley behind Num-Ti-Jah Lodge, the Bow Glacier is the same glacier that originally carved out the entire Bow Valley (which you've driven through as you came

Upper Bow Lake with the Bow Glacier in the background.

Hiking on Parker Ridge with the Saskatchewan Glacier in the background.

northwest from Banff) 10,000 years ago. For a closer view, hike the 4.6km (2.9-mile) trail to Bow Glacier Falls, which starts just behind Num-Ti-Jah Lodge. *36km (22 miles) north of Lake Louise on Hwy. 93.*

⑥ Snowbird Glacier. Clinging to the east face of Mt. Patterson, just north of Bow Pass, the beautiful Snowbird Glacier drapes over a cliff, with wings that are limited in size by the width of each ledge. Only the left wing is visible from the highway, best seen 3.1km (2 miles) north of the Silverhorn Creek Bridge, on the west side of the highway at the bottom of the hill past Bow Summit. *48km (30 miles) north of Lake Louise on Hwy. 93.*

⑦ Saskatchewan Glacier. The longest tongue of ice flowing off the

Tourists climb the Columbia Icefield.

Columbia Icefield, this is a classic outlet valley glacier. The best view is from Parkers Ridge, a superb 2.7km (1.7-mile) hike up the ridge from the highway. *117km (73 miles) north of Lake Louise on Hwy. 93. See p 146.*

⑧ Columbia Icefield. The largest frozen ice mass south of the Arctic Circle, this icefield measures 325 sq. km (125 sq. miles). It includes six glaciers: Athabasca, Saskatchewan, Dome, Columbia, Castleguard, and Stutfield. *125km (78 miles) north of Lake Louise on Hwy. 93. See p 99 for more information on experiencing the icefield.*

⑨ Athabasca Glacier. The most famous glacier in North America is in Jasper National Park. It's also the easiest glacier to access—more than 10,000 people visit this frozen river of ice each busy summer day. *125km (78 miles) north of Lake Louise on Hwy. 93. See p 99.*

⑩ Snow Dome. Also in Jasper National Park, this peak is a hydrological apex. One of only two such places in the world, water flows in three directions: north to the Arctic Ocean, east to the Atlantic Ocean, and west to the Pacific Ocean. The Dome Glacier can be seen on Snow Dome's north side as you approach the Columbia Icefield from the north on Hwy. 93.

B anff is no zoo! Here, animals roam free, and the natural rhythms of the wilderness are maintained. There are 53 species of wild mammals in Banff, 13 of which are on Parks Canada's "Species at Risk" list. Count yourself lucky if you catch any wildlife sightings in Banff. But if you follow this list, your chances will be higher. Dawn and dusk are the best times of day for spotting wildlife. Be sure to keep track, and report all wildlife sightings to Parks Canada at ☎ 403/762-1470. START: **Town of Banff.**

Wildlife in Banff National Park:

❶ Urban Elk in the Town of Banff. During certain times of the year (mainly spring and summer), elk make their way into the heart of the Town of Banff. The drive around the Banff Springs Golf Course is a prime area for spotting these magnificent mammals. *At the end of Golf Course Dr. past Bow Falls.*

❷ Minnewanka Loop. Just northeast of the Town of Banff, the drive along the Minnewanka Road is particularly good for seeing bighorn sheep who often gather near Two Jack Lake, 12km (7½ miles) from the Town of Banff on Minnewanka Loop. *Take Banff Ave. to the northeast out of town. It turns into Minnewanka Loop after going under the Trans-Canada Hwy. 1.*

❸ Muleshoe. An open pasture off the Bow Valley Parkway Hwy. 1A, this is a good spot for coyotes, elk, and mule deer. Birders also come here to spot Western Tanagers and Hammond's flycatchers. *Take the Trans-Canada Hwy. 1, 5.5km (3½ miles) west of Banff to the Bow Valley Pkwy. (Hwy. 1A) Continue for 5.5km (3½ miles) to Muleshoe Picnic Area.*

❹ Bourgeau Wildlife Overpass. This is one of six specially-designed tree-covered bridges that go over the Trans-Canada Hwy. 1 west of Banff and allow wildlife like bears, elk, coyotes, wolves, cougars, and moose to roam freely in their natural habitat. They're aimed to reduce the large number of mammals (and humans) that were being killed by vehicles, and they've been

Elk often make their way into the heart of town.

Bear Jams: Keep Moving, People!

Everybody's thrilled to catch a glimpse of a bear in the wild. In the Canadian Rockies, there are more "bear jams" than "traffic jams" as tourists pile up in their vehicles to snap photos of grizzlies or black bears, creating chaos on the roads. Whistling, yelling, running about . . . tourists behave strangely in the presence of a magnificent mammal, causing problems that can turn fatal for the bear and for other drivers. If you see a bear and want a closer look, slow down safely but do not stop. Give the bear space. The moment one car stops, everybody stops. No matter the circumstances, stay in your vehicle and do not approach the bear. Once alerted to the sighting of a bear, Parks Canada staff and often the police will appear at the scene and urge travelers to keep moving. Remember to call in a bear sighting to ☎ 403/762-1470.

extremely successful. While you can't stop to take a look at the bridge, do drive slowly and keep your eyes open. There are also 38 underpasses between Banff and Lake Louise. *11km (6¾ miles) northwest of Banff on the Trans-Canada Hwy. 1.*

⑤ Helen Lake. From the high alpine environment of this hiking

Keep your eyes peeled for mountain goats perched on cliff sides at places like Mt. Coleman.

trail near the Crowfoot Glacier, you'll be tramping through prime grizzly bear habitat and may also spot white-tailed ptarmigan, grouse, and golden eagles. *33km (21 miles) north of Lake Louise on the Icefields Pkwy. See p 147.*

⑥ Bow Summit. Following the short interpretive trail to the Peyto Lake and on to the Bow Summit lookout, you may be able to see cute little mammals like pikas (which look like miniature rabbits) and hoary marmots. *41km (25 miles) north of Lake Louise on the Icefields Pkwy.*

⑦ Waterfowl Lakes. You won't be surprised to see mallard ducks and loons on these lakes. What may well surprise you, however, is spotting a moose. Summer evenings are the best time. *58km (36 miles) north of Lake Louise on the Icefields Pkwy.*

⑧ Mt. Coleman. From the picnic area at its base, mountain goats can be spotted clinging precariously to the cliff of this peak. *100km (62 miles) north of Lake Louise on the Icefields Pkwy.* ●

4 Banff National Park

The Town of Banff

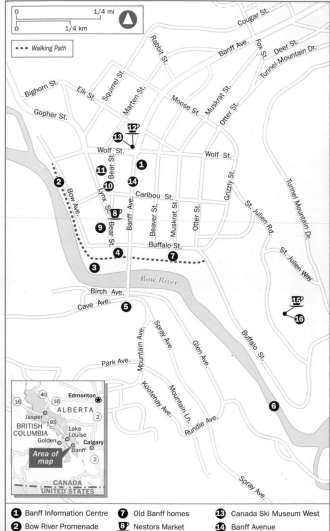

1. Banff Information Centre
2. Bow River Promenade
3. Central Park
4. Banff Park Museum
5. Cascade Gardens
6. Bow Falls
7. Old Banff homes
8. Nestors Market
9. Whyte Museum
10. Canada House Gallery
11. Old Crag Cabin
12. Cascade Plaza
13. Canada Ski Museum West
14. Banff Avenue
15. Three Ravens Wine Bar
16. The Banff Centre for the Arts

Previous page: The famous view of Banff's Moraine Lake.

The Town of Banff is the beating heart of Canada's first and most important national park. Planned and organized as a resort town from the beginning, the focus here remains on pleasing visitors. There are historic and natural highlights dotted around the outskirts of town, but the center of all things is bustling Banff Avenue, the main drag. Here, tourists speaking dozens of languages nip in and out of shops, pop into a pub for a pint, get their skis and bikes tuned up, and enjoy some truly fabulous cuisine. **START: Park your car in the parking lot behind the Banff Information Centre.**

① ★★ **Banff Information Centre.** This is a must for your first stop of the day. In the heritage building in the heart of "downtown" Banff, it's a great orientation center, with helpful desks staffed by the friendly folks at Parks Canada and the Banff-Lake Louise Tourism Bureau. They have maps, brochures, and trail updates, and they can help you decide what to do when. At the back, there's a short video that will also help you get your bearings and understand just why this place is so important. ⏲ *20 min. 224 Banff Ave.* ☎ *403/762-1550. Daily mid-May to mid-June and early Sept to late Sept 9am–7pm; mid-June to early Sept 8am–8pm; late Sept to mid-May 9am–4pm. See p 13.*

Exit the Information Centre and cross Banff Avenue at the lights at the corner of Wolf Street. Continue down Wolf Street 3 blocks, crossing Bear and Lynx streets, until you reach:

② **Bow River Promenade.** The canoe docks mark the beginning of a gentle, paved trail that follows one of Canada's most important rivers. The beautiful Bow River is the longest river in Banff National Park. From its headwaters at Bow Lake, 90km (56 miles) north of the Town of Banff, it flows south and east, passing through Banff, Canmore, and Calgary. It joins the South Saskatchewan River and eventually drains into Hudson Bay and the Atlantic Ocean, on Canada's east coast. This promenade makes for a good stroll.

Follow the trail downriver, around the bend to:

A couple enjoys a walk along the Bow River.

Canada Place's Cascade Gardens.

③ Central Park. Site of Canada Day parties, weddings, picnics, and Frisbee-tossing, this is Banff's main outdoor meeting space. During the summer, there are often outdoor concerts here, and Parks Canada's "Roving Interpreters" often set up shop at one of the picnic tables (you'll spot them in their red and green uniforms). Sometimes there are elk feeding here, too! ⏱ *15 min. Along the north shore of the Bow River btw. Banff Ave. and Bow Ave. parallel to Buffalo St.*

One of Banff's original heritage homes.

Next to the park, on the east side between the park and Banff Avenue, is:

④ kids ★★ Banff Park Museum. A beautiful building dating to 1903 and reflecting early Rocky Mountain architecture, this is the oldest natural history museum in Western Canada. It houses an incredibly complete collection of wildlife. It's also a superb rainy-day option. Come for a good look at beavers' teeth or an elk's antler. Daily tours start at 3pm. ⏱ *30 min. 91 Banff Ave. ☎ 403/762-1558. Oct 1–May 15 daily 1–5pm; May 15–Sept 30 daily 10am–6pm. Adults $3.90, seniors $3.40, youth $1.90, free for children 5 and under.*

Cross over the Bow River Bridge. Cross Mountain Road and head through the iron gate for a visit to:

⑤ Cascade Gardens. Inspired by the geological history of the Rockies, this lovely garden includes a series of fountains, or "cascades" that are an essential part of appreciating the architecture and design of the Banff Administration Building. During summer, the local Siksika First Nation erects a traditional

Some of the cheeses available at Nestor's Market.

tepee here with an interesting cultural exhibit. Turn to face Cascade Mountain and Banff Avenue for that timeless photo opportunity. 🕐 *30 min. At the T-intersection where Spray and Cave aves. meet Banff Ave., just over the Bow River Bridge. Daily 24 hr. Free admission.*

Back across Mountain Road, turn right (east) before crossing the bridge, following the trail 1.2km (.8 mile) to:

⑥ ★ Bow Falls. Tucked in beneath the Fairmont Banff Springs Hotel, **Bow Falls** will let you escape the hustle and bustle of the busy Banff Townsite. The 10m (33-ft.) falls, eroding between two rock formations, roar and wash away any tension you may have picked up. The rock on the left bank of the river is 245 million years old, while the one on the right bank is some 320 million years old. Downstream from the falls, the Banff Springs Golf Course dominates the southern side of the valley.

Walk back up river. At the Bow River Bridge, take the east (or downriver) sidewalk, and begin exploring the historic neighborhoods of "old Banff," along Buffalo and Muskrat streets.

⑦ Old Banff homes. Along Buffalo Street, backing onto the Bow River, are some of the most spectacular homes in Western Canada. Remember, Banff has a "need to reside" rule—only people with jobs or businesses in Banff can live here. At 313 Buffalo St. is a home dating to 1920 that was once the Park Superintendent's Residence. At the corner of Buffalo and Muskrat streets, you'll find the historic Grant-Hemming home, built in 1921 from local materials (note the Rundlestone steps and riverstone chimney). Next door are legendary naturalist and climatologist Norman Sanson's home and the summer residence of Senator Amedée Forget.

8 If you were drawn to one of the riverside picnic tables along the Bow River, drop into **Nestor's Market.** With a deli, bakery, and plenty of fresh produce, you can put together a superb lunch to go. *122 Bear St.* ☎ *403/762-3663. Daily 8am–11pm. $.*

Walk back to the Bow River trail at the end of Muskrat Street, and continue along the river, passing Central Park. On Lynx Street, turn right to:

Old Crag Cabin, built in the 19th century.

⑨ ★★ Whyte Museum of the Canadian Rockies. This museum houses excellent exhibits about the human history of Banff and has a tremendously wealthy archive of memoirs, sketches, photographs, and personal artifacts of Rocky Mountain pioneers, visionaries, and artists. Changing exhibits shine light on how the mountains have inspired generations; the newest is Gateway to the Rockies, which looks at local history with interactive displays.

The entrance to Banff's Whyte Museum.

Another excellent rainy-day activity. ⏱ *90 min. 111 Bear St.* ☎ *403/762-2291. Daily 10am–5pm. Admission $8 adults, $5 seniors and students, free for children 6 and under.*

Cross Lynx Street and head down the lovely Bear Street. On the left-hand side, a few shops down, you'll find:

⑩ ★ Canada House Gallery. Even if you aren't a dedicated art collector, it's worth taking time to explore this fine arts shop and gallery. Featuring exclusively Canadian art, the focus is on landscape, contemporary, and Native styles. It's not hard to understand how the Rockies inspire these artists. There are often opening receptions for the public on Saturday afternoons. ⏱ *20 min. 201 Bear St.* ☎ *403/762-3757. Sun–Thurs 9:30am–6pm; Fri–Sat 9:30am–7pm. www.canada house.com.*

⑪ Old Crag Cabin. Built between 1888 and 1890, this tiny wooden cabin is one of the most storied buildings in Banff. Home to the weekly newspaper from 1901 to 1929, it was restored and relocated in 1999 and is now the "downtown" home and box office for the Banff Centre. Pop in to see what's on! 🕐 5 min. 211 Bear St. ☎ 403/762-6301. Tues–Sun 11am–6pm.

Follow Bear Street to its terminus at Wolf Street and head into:

12 **Cascade Plaza.** For a quick and affordable pick-me-up, jump into the food court at the basement of Banff's biggest mall. You'll find a dozen different counters serving everything from sushi and pizza to curries. You can buy lunch for under $8. *317 Banff Ave.* ☎ *403/762-8484. $.*

Before riding the escalators up, start at the bottom floor display for:

13 **Canadian Ski Museum West.** From early wooden telemark skis to the latest World Cup victories, the history of Banff's favorite sport is told in displays throughout the three-story Cascade Mall. Start at the first floor and work your way up to follow in chronological order. You may even bump into a real ski legend or two while roaming about Banff. 🕐 20 min. 317 Banff Ave. ☎ 403/762-8484. Mon–Thurs 10am–7pm; Fri–Sat 10am–9pm; Sun 11am–7pm. Free admission.

Exit the mall and turn right to stroll:

14 **Banff Avenue.** Home to great shops, cafes, restaurants, historic buildings, and a general hustle-and-bustle, take time to stroll the scene and eavesdrop on dozens of languages on one of Canada's iconic main drags. A massive redevelopment project in 2007 widened the sidewalks and made street life more pleasant.

Head up Wolf Street and turn right up St. Julien Road. Follow the curving road until you enter the campus of the Banff Centre.

An opera performance at the Banff Centre.

15 ★ **Three Ravens Wine Bar.** For a quick pre-concert bite to eat or a cocktail, or a post-event glass of wine and dessert, you can't beat this scenic restaurant above the Sally Borden Building in the Banff Centre. It wins for the best restaurant view in Banff, by far. Try a glass of pinot noir from the Okanagan with Spanish paprika beef rolls. *At the Banff Centre on St. Julien Rd.* ☎ *403/762-6300. Daily 4pm–midnight. $$.*

16 **The Banff Centre.** Part of the town's fabric for nearly a century, this is a world-renowned arts, culture, and educational institution that hosts celebrated musicians, writers, and other artists from around the world on a regular basis. The Centre's Summer Arts Festival showcases the best in a variety of artistic areas—from costume design and creative writing, to drama and opera, to jazz and classical music. It's another place where the mountains truly awaken inspiration and creativity. Don't miss the chance to take in a truly inspiring performance, often in the outdoors, during your visit to Banff. *St. Julien Rd.* ☎ *403/762-6100. www.banffcentre.ca.*

Lake Minnewanka

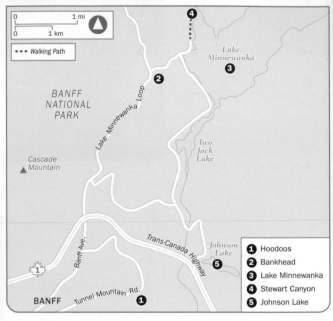

0   1 mi
0   1 km

••• Walking Path

BANFF NATIONAL PARK

Cascade ▲ Mountain

Lake Minnewanka Loop

②

④

Lake Minnewanka

③

Two Jack Lake

Trans-Canada Highway

Banff Ave.

Johnson Lake

⑤

BANFF

Tunnel Mountain Rd.

①

① Hoodoos
② Bankhead
③ Lake Minnewanka
④ Stewart Canyon
⑤ Johnson Lake

S ome call it a giant bathtub, but **Lake Minnewanka** does offer unique activities and a chance for open skies. It's the biggest lake in Banff National Park, created by nature and later expanded by humanity. The Minnewanka Loop makes a nice tour from the Town of Banff and can be done in a leisurely 2 or 3 hours. To extend it, add in the hike to C-Level Cirque or another of the hikes listed in chapter 6. Watch for big-horn sheep on the road near Two Jack Lake—and remember not to feed them. **START: Town of Banff. Head east off Banff Avenue onto Tunnel Mountain Road.**

---

① Hoodoos. The mysterious pillars look like they've been dropped from outer space. In fact, they are free-standing posts made of silt, gravel, and rocks cemented together by dissolved limestone. The uncemented particles were slowly eroded and washed away. There is a paved, stroller-friendly 500m (1,640-ft.) trail to a nice viewpoint that also offers lovely views of Mt. Rundle and the Bow River. *Just off Tunnel Mountain*

Rd. past the entrance to Tunnel Mountain Campground Village I, 4km (2½ miles) east of Banff.

Tunnel Mountain Road continues to loop around until it meets up with Lake Minnewanka Road again, which passes under the Trans-Canada Highway (Hwy. 1) and goes northeast along the side of Cascade Mountain. Pull

Lake Minnewanka used to be known as "The Lake of the Water Spirits."

off Lake Minnewanka Road after 3km (1¾ miles).

❷ Bankhead. Once the working center of Banff, Bankhead was a small settlement that boomed in the early 20th century. Old machinery and foundations are still in place, such as the entranceway to the former church and the transformer building, which features a display about coal mining. A short 10 minute walk about the area, following interpretive displays, will help bring the history to life.

Continue down the road another 2.6km (1½ miles) and pull into the large parking lot just before:

❸ Lake Minnewanka. This lake used to be called "The Lake of the Water Spirits" by the Stoney Nation, who apparently feared these spirits and refused to swim in or boat on the lake. Early Europeans took a like-

Mt. Rundle, the Bow River, and the Hoodoos from the Hoodoo Trail Overlook.

wise timid view, calling it "Devil's Lake." Although it's too cold for a dip, boaters today have no fear. This is the only lake in Banff where motorboats are allowed. From May through October, you can take an enclosed boat trip to the end of the lake. ⏱ *90 min.* ☎ *403/762-3473. www.explorerockies.com. $44 adults, $20 children 6–15, free for children 5 and under.*

To the north of the parking lot is a day-use area with picnic tables and shelters. Continue through to reach the trail for Stewart Canyon.

❹ ★ Stewart Canyon. A nice 30-minute round-trip walk along the lakeshore takes you to this canyon, named for the first superintendent of Banff National Park. Much of the canyon has lain underwater since Minnewanka was dammed, first in 1895 and again in 1912 and 1941. The highlight is the giant wooden truss bridge. The trail is very accessible (even to wheelchairs).

Returning to the parking lot, head across the causeway, past Two Jack Lake. At 2.4km (1½ miles) from Minnewanka, turn left to:

❺ Johnson Lake. Not to be confused with Johnston Canyon, which is farther west, this man-made lake is perhaps the best place for a swim on a hot day. A 3.5km (2.1-mile) trail circles the lake; walk counterclockwise to take in views of Cascade Mountain.

Bow Valley Parkway

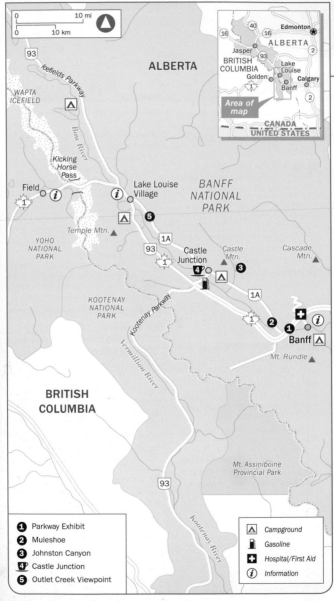

| Scale: | 0 — 10 mi / 0 — 10 km |

ALBERTA

Icefields Parkway 93

WAPTA ICEFIELD

Bow River

Kicking Horse Pass

Field (i) 1

Lake Louise Village (i)

BANFF NATIONAL PARK

5 Outlet Creek Viewpoint

Temple Mtn.

YOHO NATIONAL PARK

1A

93

1

Castle Junction **4**

Castle Mtn. **3**

Cascade Mtn.

1A

KOOTENAY NATIONAL PARK

Kootenay Parkway

1

2 **1** Banff

Mt. Rundle

Vermillion River

BRITISH COLUMBIA

Mt. Assiniboine Provincial Park

93

Kootenay River

Inset map:
16 40 16 **Edmonton**
ALBERTA
Jasper 2
93
BRITISH COLUMBIA
Golden Lake Louise
1 Banff **Calgary**
2
Area of map
CANADA
UNITED STATES

Legend

1 Parkway Exhibit
2 Muleshoe
3 Johnston Canyon
4 Castle Junction
5 Outlet Creek Viewpoint

Campground
Gasoline
Hospital/First Aid
(i) Information

The Bow Valley Parkway (Hwy. 1A) is less congested than the Trans-Canada Hwy. 1, although the two roads run parallel along the Bow River. Built in 1920—the first road connecting Banff and Lake Louise—this 51km (32-mile) route still feels more like a mountain road than an expressway. The 13 interpretive stops along the way are all worthwhile. I've selected the best of the bunch. The drive will take about 3 hours, including stops. **START: Town of Banff.**

Head left (north) on Mt. Norquay Road out of the townsite and turn left (west) onto the Trans-Canada Highway (Hwy. 1). You'll meet up with the Bow Valley Parkway about 5km (3 miles) from town.

1 Parkway Exhibit. Westbound travelers can make a quick stop at this turnoff to orient themselves to the route ahead. There is a good map and a refresher on the etiquette of wildlife encounters. *.9km (½ mile) from start of Bow Valley Pkwy.*

2 ★ Muleshoe. A short 1km (.6 mile) trail starts across the highway from the picnic area and explores the remnants of the 1993 prescribed fire. *5.5km (3½ miles) from start of Bow Valley Pkwy.*

3 ★ Johnston Canyon. A walkway leads up this canyon, past two large waterfalls carved through limestone bedrock. The first part of the trail is on a paved surface and is a very gentle climb that ends at the first waterfall, called the Lower Falls. There are interpretive signs on the way up to the Upper Falls, almost twice the height of the Lower Falls and a farther 1.6km (1 mile). *18km (11 miles) west of Banff Townsite.*

4 Castle Junction. Three important roads meet here—the Bow Valley Parkway, Hwy. 93, and the Trans-Canada Hwy. 1. There's a gas station, a small convenience store, and cozy cabins. If you haven't already done so in the Banff Townsite, this is a good place to pick up basic picnic supplies. *28km (17 miles) from the Town of Banff.* ☎ 403/522-2783. *$.*

5 Outlet Creek Viewpoint. Here you'll find a grand view of towering Mt. Temple, the third highest peak in Banff National Park. Known as Morant's Curve, the S-bend in the Canadian Pacific Railway tracks below here offers a classic photo when eastbound trains motor through the valley. *46km (29 miles) from the start of the Bow Valley Pkwy.*

The 98-foot high upper falls of Johnston Canyon.

Lake Louise

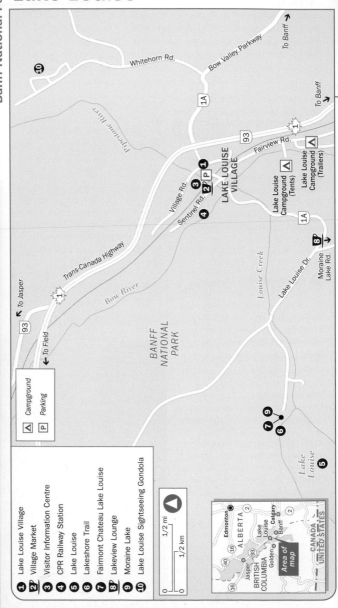

Whitehorn Rd.
Bow Valley Parkway
To Banff

Pipestone River

1A

93
To Banff

Fairview Rd.

Village Rd.

LAKE LOUISE VILLAGE

3 1
P
2
4

Sentinel Rd.

Lake Louise Campground (Tents)

Lake Louise Campground (Trailers)

1A

Trans-Canada Highway

Louise Creek

8

Moraine Lake Rd.

Lake Louise Dr.

To Jasper

93

To Field

Bow River

BANFF NATIONAL PARK

7 9
6

5

Lake Louise

△ Campground
P Parking

1 Lake Louise Village
2 Village Market
3 Visitor Information Centre
4 CPR Railway Station
5 Lake Louise
6 Lakeshore Trail
7 Fairmont Chateau Lake Louise
8 Lakeview Lounge
9 Moraine Lake
10 Lake Louise Sightseeing Gondola

1/2 mi

1/2 km

0

ALBERTA

Edmonton

2

Lake Louise
Calgary
Banff

2

Jasper

93

Golden

16

BRITISH COLUMBIA

16

40

Area of map

CANADA
UNITED STATES

You can't come to Banff and not see placid, beautiful Lake Louise. Situated 56km (35 miles) northwest of the Town of Banff, Lake Louise is perhaps the most photographed lake in the country, one that people from all over the world associate with their image of Canada. It's also the name of the small village just below the lake. While many people drive out just to snap a photo and then return to their hotel, it deserves a full day, with at least a short hike and time for tea. **START: Lake Louise Village parking lot.**

Travel Tip

Leave your car at the village parking lot and board the shuttle up to Lake Louise if you want to avoid parking headaches at the always-packed lakeside lot. The shuttle, however, won't take you to Moraine Lake.

1 Lake Louise Village. Consisting of the key elements of a small village (or "hamlet," as Parks Canada refers to it), here you'll find gas stations, a grocery and liquor store, post office, some apartments, an ATM, restaurants, a bookshop, and an outdoor equipment store. And let's not forget some outstanding hotels—which, admittedly, you might not expect to find in a small village or "hamlet." *See p 78 for Lake Louise hotels.*

2 **Village Market.** Amid the trail maps and souvenirs, this grocery store also has picnic supplies. Although it's not as well stocked as the grocery stores in Banff, you can get some dips, veggies, simple sandwiches, snacks, and drinks to fill your backpack. ☎ *403/522-3894. 101 Lake Louise Dr. $.*

3 ★ Visitor Information Centre. Housed behind Samson Mall, Parks Canada's main outpost in Lake Louise has a ton of information, including exhibits and a theater presenting the geological history of the Canadian Rockies. You can also pick up permits and maps, as well as trail, weather, and road reports. *101 Lake Louise Dr.* ☎ *403/522-3833. Daily Sept 3–Apr 30 9am–4pm; May 1–June 18 9am–5pm; June 19–Sept 2 8:30am–7pm.*

Inside a Samson Mall shop in Lake Louise Village.

The History of the Chateau

The Chateau Lake Louise had humble beginnings, in the form of a cabin built on the site in 1890 by the CPR (Canadian Pacific Railway). By 1917 the cabin had burned to the ground, and a hotel with all the modern amenities of the day was erected in its place. While the Banff Springs Hotel, also run by the CPR, was to be luxurious, the CPR marketed the Chateau Lake Louise as a destination for outdoor adventurers. Mountaineers, artists, and horseback riders flooded in, giving the Chateau a level of popularity and character that the Springs is still striving for. With a feel akin to the Swiss Alps, mountain culture is alive and well here.

Follow Lake Louis Drive through the 4-way stop, pass beneath the railway overpass, and turn right immediately onto Sentinel Drive. Follow this road for 1.4km (¾ mile).

❹ **CPR Railway Station.** The oldest building in Lake Louise is the log station across the tracks from the village core. Built in 1910, it was a working terminal for more than 60 years. A National Historic Site, the station is now home to a restaurant in summertime. (*No street no.*) *Sentinel Rd.* ☎ *403/522-2600.*

It's about 8km (5 miles) or a 5-minute drive from the village up to the lake itself and the often-crowded parking lot.

❺ ★★★ **Lake Louise.** In summer, thousands of people empty out of bus tours in front of the lake each day to have their picture taken, then jump back on to the bus, and head off to the next tour stop. It's quite crowded. But the lake is so beautiful and pristine, you should go anyway. Fed by glacial meltwater, Lake Louise is 2.4km (1½ miles) long, 500m (1,640 ft.) wide, and 90m (295 ft.) deep. Behind it is **Mt. Victoria,** at an elevation of 3,464m (11,365 ft.), with the thick **Victoria Glacier** on its front ridge. The lake was named after Princess Louise Caroline Alberta (1849–1939), the fourth daughter of Queen Victoria and later the wife of the governor-general of Canada.

❻ ★ **Lakeshore Trail.** This is a 2km (1.2-mile) path (each way) that runs from the Chateau along the

Inside the Lakeview Lounge at Chateau Lake Louise.

A hiker takes a break overlooking Moraine Lake.

lake's north shore to the western end of the lake. At the back of the lake, quartzite crags are popular with rock climbers. It's open to walkers May through October, and to skiers the rest of the year.

❼ ★ Fairmont Chateau Lake Louise. Often called a "diamond in the wilderness," this is an impressive and important hotel rich in history and obviously blessed with an incredible setting. If you aren't a guest, you are welcome to come in for a meal, some shopping, or tea, or just to roam and wonder at the fantastic ambience. *See p 80.*

❽ It's all quite civilized inside the **Lakeview Lounge**, a superb place for an afternoon tea at the Chateau Lake Louise. The view, stretching across the lake, is divine. Traditional afternoon tea service includes sandwiches, scones, sweets, and polished silver. ☎ *403/522-1818. Tea served daily noon–4pm. $$$.*

There is a winding road (open only May–Oct) that takes you the 13km (8 miles) from Lake Louise to Moraine Lake. At the often-crowded parking lot are a lodge, a picnic area, and some interpretive exhibits.

❾ ★★★ Moraine Lake. Just south of Lake Louise is another stunning alpine lake, situated in front of the Valley of the Ten Peaks. Wild and dramatic, Moraine Lake is very popular. You can rent canoes here for $35/hour, or walk an excellent interpretive trail to the Moraine Lake Rockpile for the view that used to be on the Canadian $20 bill. Moraine Lake is also the trail head for a number of the best hikes in Banff National Park (see chapter 6).

Head back to the Lake Louise Road, down to the village, over the Trans-Canada Hwy. 1 and up Whitehorn Road to:

❿ ★★ kids Lake Louise Sightseeing Gondola. Take a gondola to the summit of Whitehorn Mountain for excellent views of the Bow Valley, Lake Louise, and the Continental Divide. Naturalists lead guided hikes that are great interactive learning experiences. Grizzly bears have been known to hang out here in the summer, so going with a guide is a wise idea. *At the top of Whitehorn Rd.* ☎ *403/522-3555. www.lakelouisegondola.com. May 15–June 22 Mon–Fri 9:30am–4pm; June 23–July 31 daily 9:30am–5:30pm; Aug 1–Sept 9 daily 9am–6:30pm; Sept 10–Sept 30 daily 9:30am–4:30pm. $28 adult, $14 child 6–15, free for kids 5 and under.*

The **Icefields Parkway**

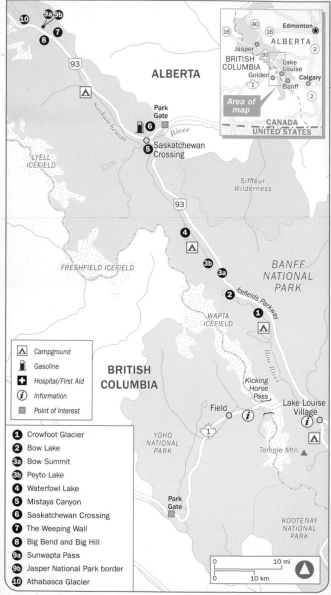

ALBERTA

Park Gate

Saskatchewan
River

Saskatchewan
Crossing

*Siffleur
Wilderness*

*LYELL
ICEFIELD*

FRESHFIELD ICEFIELD

*BANFF
NATIONAL
PARK*

Icefields Parkway

*WAPTA
ICEFIELD*

**BRITISH
COLUMBIA**

Bow River

*Kicking
Horse
Pass*

Lake Louise
Village

Field

*YOHO
NATIONAL
PARK*

Temple Mtn.

Park
Gate

*KOOTENAY
NATIONAL
PARK*

Area of
map

CANADA
UNITED STATES

Edmonton
ALBERTA
Jasper
BRITISH
COLUMBIA
Golden
Lake
Louise
Banff
Calgary

◭	Campground
⛽	Gasoline
✚	Hospital/First Aid
ⓘ	Information
■	Point of Interest

1 Crowfoot Glacier
2 Bow Lake
3a Bow Summit
3b Peyto Lake
4 Waterfowl Lake
5 Mistaya Canyon
6 Saskatchewan Crossing
7 The Weeping Wall
8 Big Bend and Big Hill
9a Sunwapta Pass
9b Jasper National Park border
10 Athabasca Glacier

0   10 mi
0   10 km

The landscape you see on the spectacular Icefields Parkway is the kind that used to dominate western North America. Hwy. 93, the Icefields Parkway, connects Banff and Jasper National Parks, and along the way you'll be wowed by raging rivers, turquoise lakes, glacier-clad summits, and massive icefields. The hiking trails and the wildlife viewing are outstanding. Plan to get out of your car often! This tour only covers the highway as far as the Icefields Centre. For information on continuing on to Jasper, see p 98. START: **Lake Louise.**

Travel Tip

If you haven't already got one, pick up a detailed map and guide to the Icefields Parkway from the Lake Louise Visitors Centre, in Lake Louise's Samson Mall (101 Lake Louise Dr.; ☎ 403/522-3833).

Continuing north on the Icefields Parkway, the road steadily climbs higher and higher and the views become more and more dramatic as you make your way through three river valleys and pass beneath towering glacier-topped peaks.

1 Crowfoot Glacier is the first of a long lineup of glaciers you'll see. There are interpretive signs posted at the roadside viewpoint. It's a good spot to contemplate the shrinking of the world's glaciers and the impact of climate change. *33km (21 miles) north of the Trans-Canada Hwy. 1 junction at Lake Louise.*

2 ★ Bow Lake. This ice-blue lake is the third-largest in Banff National Park. Almost all of its water is glacier-fed; you can just see the Bow Glacier at the back of the lake. It's a nice place for a picnic. The red-roofed inn on the lake's northeast shore is Num-Ti-Jah Lodge (p 81). *34km (21 miles) north of the Trans-Canada Hwy. 1 junction at Lake Louise.*

3 ★★ Bow Summit and Peyto Lake. At an elevation of 2,069m (6,788 ft.), you're at the highest point in Canada that can be crossed by a highway year-round. Walk the short interpretive trail at Bow Summit to see this beautiful turquoise lake set far below the lookout in a deep glacial valley. It's named for pioneer guide "Wild" Bill Peyto, who was a warden in Banff National Park. Continue farther along a short

Sunrise at Crowfoot Mountain and Crowfoot Glacier.

Bow Lake, the third-largest in Banff National Park.

extension of the trail, going left and up the hill, for views of the glacier that feeds the lake. *40km (25 miles) north of the Trans-Canada Hwy. 1 junction at Lake Louise.*

Heading north past Peyto Lake, the landscape becomes more barren and beautiful.

4 Waterfowl Lake. Stop at the pullout next to this serene lake to view some of the mighty peaks along the Continental Divide. In fact, all of the mountains on the west side of the Icefields Parkway form part of

The Mistaya River descends through Mistaya Canyon.

the backbone of the continent. From here, you can see Howse Peak and Mt. Chephren, a classically horned peak resembling a pyramid. *56km (35 miles) north of the Trans-Canada Hwy. 1 junction at Lake Louise.*

5 ★ Mistaya Canyon. Deep and steep, the beauty of this canyon is in its sublimely curvy walls, the fierce roar of the water, and in the quiet trail, much quieter than at the other famous canyons in the Rockies. The Mistaya River drops off Bow Summit and has carved out a series of potholes along the canyon's walls. A steep but short .5km (.3-mile) trail leads from the north end of a parking lot on the west side of the Icefields Parkway down into to the canyon. *71km (44 miles) north of the Trans-Canada Hwy. 1 junction at Lake Louise.*

6 Saskatchewan Crossing. On the banks of the Saskatchewan River, there is a warden station, gas station, snack bar, and gift shop at a basic roadside complex called "The Crossing." It's a good place to get out and stretch your legs. *77km (48 miles) north of the Trans-Canada Hwy. 1 junction with the start of the Icefields Pkwy. 93.*

Pull over on the west side of the highway to get a look at:

7 The Weeping Wall. In summer you may see only a few drops of water wetting the ridge on the east side of the highway, but in the winter these drips and drops freeze to create a huge frozen waterfall draped in layer upon layer of ice. This is a hot spot for the technical sport of ice climbing. *106km (66 miles) north of the Trans-Canada Hwy. 1 junction at Lake Louise.*

8 Big Bend and Big Hill. A famous hairpin turn is followed by a steep hill, both of which are excruciatingly difficult for cyclists. There is a pullout at the top of the hill with a nice view of Bridal View Falls. *111km (69 miles) north of the Trans-Canada Hwy. 1 junction at Lake Louise.*

9 Sunwapta Pass and Jasper National Park. At 2,023m (6,637 ft.), this is the second-highest point on the Icefields Parkway and forms the border between Banff and Jasper national parks. It's also the border between the two watersheds: The North Saskatchewan River drains from here to Lake Winnipeg, Hudson Bay, and the Atlantic Ocean, while on the other side of the pass the Sunwapta River eventually makes its way to the Arctic Ocean. It's all downhill from here—108km (67 miles) north on the Icefields Parkway to Jasper Townsite. *122km (76 miles) north of the Trans-Canada Hwy. 1 junction at Lake Louise.*

Water streaming down the Weeping Wall.

10 ★★ Athabasca Glacier. With its tongue almost touching the highway, this is the most accessible of the six principal glaciers that make up the Columbia Icefield and is also the most visited glacier in North America. It's receding 2 to 3m (6½–9¾ ft.) each year. Park your car at the Toe-of-the-Glacier trail head (which was covered by ice in the 1950s) and walk down through the lunar-like landscape to the ice. Don't venture onto the ice without a guide (see sidebar). For information on the Columbia Icefield and the "snocoach" tours, see below. *127km (79 miles) north of the Trans-Canada Hwy. 1 junction at Lake Louise.*

Icewalk Interpretive Tours

More adventurous folk will prefer to join a certified mountain guide who leaves daily from the Toe-of-the-Glacier parking lot for guided hikes that allow you to walk on the ice. Three- to 4-hour hikes cost $70 for adults and $35 for kids 7 to 16 (kids 6 and under not allowed). More strenuous—and more exploratory—6-hour hikes cost $85 for adults, $45 for kids 7 to 16. Call ☎ 800/565-7547 or see www.icewalks.com.

Dining in **Banff National Park**

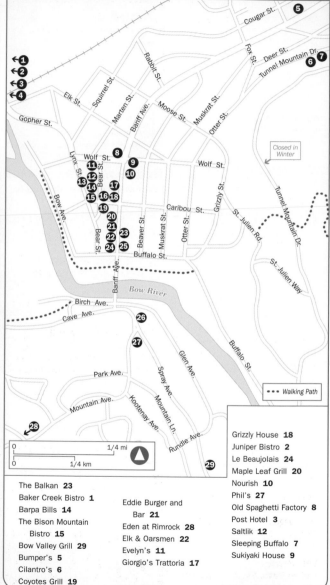

The Balkan **23**
Baker Creek Bistro **1**
Barpa Bills **14**
The Bison Mountain
   Bistro **15**
Bow Valley Grill **29**
Bumper's **5**
Cilantro's **6**
Coyotes Grill **19**

Eddie Burger and
   Bar **21**
Eden at Rimrock **28**
Elk & Oarsmen **22**
Evelyn's **11**
Giorgio's Trattoria **17**

Grizzly House **18**
Juniper Bistro **2**
Le Beaujolais **24**
Maple Leaf Grill **20**
Nourish **10**
Phil's **27**
Old Spaghetti Factory **8**
Post Hotel **3**
Saltlik **12**
Sleeping Buffalo **7**
Sukiyaki House **9**

Dining Best Bets

Best for Adventurous Kids
Grizzly House $$ *207 Banff Ave. (p 73)*

Best Bakery
Wild Flour Bakery $ *211 Bear St. (p 75)*

Best Breakfast
★★ Coyotes Grill $$ *206 Caribou St. (p 72)*

Best Brunch
★★ Bow Valley Grill $$ *In the Fairmont Banff Springs Hotel. 405 Spray Ave. (p 71)*

Best Burger
★ Eddie Burger and Bar $ *137C Banff Ave. (p 72)*

Best Canadiana Cool
★★ Maple Leaf Grill $$ *137 Banff Ave. (p 74)*

Best Charcuterie Plate
★ Sleeping Buffalo $$$ *700 Tunnel Mountain Rd., at the Buffalo Mountain Lodge (p 75)*

Best Cheap Bowl of Hot Soup
Chaya $ *118 Banff Ave. (p 71)*

Best for Health Freaks
Nourish $$ *215 Banff Ave., second floor (p 74)*

Best Italian
★ Giorgio's Trattoria $$ *219 Banff Ave. (p 73)*

Best for Locavores
★★ The Bison $$$ *211 Bear St. (p 71)*

Best for Parents with No Babysitter
Old Spaghetti Factory $ *Cascade Plaza, 317 Banff Ave., second floor (p 74)*

Best Patio
Juniper Bistro $ *In the Juniper Hotel, bottom of Mt. Norquay Rd. (p 73)*

Best Pizza
★★ Bear Street Tavern $$ *211 Bear St. (p 70)*

Best Pub Food
★ Elk & Oarsmen $$ *Upstairs, 119 Banff Ave. (p 72)*

Best Salad Bar
Bumper's $ *603 Banff Ave. (p 71)*

Best Splurge
★★ Eden $$$ *In the Rimrock Resort Hotel, Mountain Ave. (p 72)*

Best Steakhouse
★★ Saltlik $$ *221 Bear St. (p 75)*

Best Sushi
Sukiyaki House $$ *In the Park Avenue Mall, 211 Banff Ave., second floor (p 75)*

Best Takeout
Barpa Bills $ *233 Bear St. (p 70)*

Best Wine Cellar
★★★ Post Hotel $$$ *200 Pipestone (p 74)*

Best Place Worth the Drive from Banff
★★★ Baker Creek Bistro $$ *11km (6¾ miles) southeast of Lake Louise and 14km (8¾ miles) north of Castle Junction on the Bow Valley Pkwy., Hwy. 1A. (p 70)*

Seafood from Maple Leaf Grille.

Restaurants A to Z

★★★ **Baker Creek Bistro** LAKE LOUISE *REGIONAL*   Fresh and modern food is served by warm and friendly folks inside a heritage cabin just south of Lake Louise. It's definitely worth the drive from Banff and makes a great pit stop on your way to Lake Louise or the Icefields Parkway. *11km (6¾ miles) southeast of Lake Louise and 14km (8¾ miles) north of Castle Junction on the Bow Valley Pkwy., Hwy. 1A.* ☎ *403/522-2182. www.bakercreekbistro.com. Entrees $18–$33. AE, MC, V. Daily noon–3pm and 5–9pm. Map p 68.*

kids **The Balkan** BANFF *GREEK*   The recipes at this family-owned Banff landmark come from the old country—souvlaki, moussaka, arni psito, and donair pitas (great for lunch). This is a great place for sharing. A new decor oozes Mediterranean sunshine. On Tuesdays and most Thursdays, the place comes alive with belly-dancing and plate-smashing. *120 Banff Ave.* ☎ *403/762-3454. www.banffbalkan. ca. Entrees $14–$29. AE, MC, V. Daily 11am–11pm. Map p 68.*

Barpa Bills BANFF *GREEK*   For something "to go," you can't beat a souvlaki in a warm pita, hot off the grill at this little Bear Street joint. It's topped with fresh tzatziki sauce and cooked to order. There are also gyros, burgers, and poutine, a French-Canadian specialty. Grab a stool at the counter if you want to eat in, but don't expect friendly chatter with the staff! *233 Bear St.* ☎ *403/762-0377. www.barpabills. com. Entrees $8–$14. No credit cards. Daily 11am–9pm. Map p 68.*

★★ **Bear Street Tavern** BANFF *PIZZA*   For a bite and pint with friends after skiing or biking, this happening spot is my first choice in town. The thin-crust pizza is superbly good—try the Wheeler Hut with wild mushrooms, pine nuts, truffle oil, and pesto. They also have gluten-free pizza. For something hearty, try the pork belly macaroni and cheese. There's a great wine list and daily cocktail specials. *211 Bear St., main floor.* ☎ *403/762-2021. www.bearstreettavern.ca. Entrees $11–$17. AE, MC, V. Daily 11:30am– midnight. Map p 68.*

The Bison Mountain Bistro, home to "Rocky Mountain comfort food."

A dish from the Fairmont Banff Springs' Bow Valley Grill.

★★ **The Bison** BANFF *REGIONAL* Regional and seasonal "Rocky Mountain comfort food" is perfectly suited for Banff. The classic dish is grilled bison rib steak. Or try daily game. Everything except the pickles and mayonnaise is made from scratch. The outdoor patio is the nicest in town. *211 Bear St., upstairs.* ☎ *403/ 762-5550. www.thebison.ca. Entrees $16–$45. AE, MC, V. Mon–Fri 11am– 10:30pm; Sat–Sun 10am–10:30pm. Map p 68.*

★★ **Bow Valley Grill** BANFF *CANADIAN* With an open concept kitchen and a gorgeous setting inside the Fairmont Banff Springs, this is the best brunch in town. Summertime brings market-style buffets. In wintertime, it's a la carte. *In the Fairmont Banff Springs Hotel, 405 Spray Ave.* ☎ *403/762-6860. www. fairmont.com/banffsprings. Entrees $28–$42. AE, DC, DISC, MC, V. Daily 7am–11pm, 6–9pm; Sat brunch 11:30am–1:30pm; Sun brunch 11am–2pm. Map p 68.*

kids Bumper's BANFF *STEAK-HOUSE* If a place has been serving visitors Alberta beef at affordable prices since 1975, it's got to be on to something good. Simple meals

star Alberta beef: Prime rib, a half-dozen cuts of steak, and baby back ribs are the usual go-to choices. They also have the best salad bar in town. *603 Banff Ave.* ☎ *403/ 762-2622. www.bumpersinn.com. Entrees $14–$40. AE, MC, V. Daily 5–10pm. Map p 68.*

Chaya BANFF *ASIAN* After a few hours in the fresh air, the big bowls of steaming Asian soups at Chaya hit the spot. This small spot next to McDonald's is as popular with Banff's quite large Japanese-Canadian population as it is with tourists. Try the Udon noodles or teriyaki rice bowls. The miso ramen bowl comes with ground pork and has a nice spicy kick. It's very small inside and it can be tough to get a table in peak hours. *118 Banff Ave.* ☎ *403/ 760-0882. Entrees $10–$14. Daily 11:30am–8pm. No credit card info.*

★ **Cilantro's** BANFF *CALIFORNIAN* Next to the Buffalo Mountain Lodge, this is a cozy cafe, perfect on a warm summer's evening. Pizzas from the apple-wood-fired oven are the best items on the menu, with

The luxurious Eden at Rimrock.

Evelyn's is a favorite for coffee or lunch.

deep crusts and creative ingredients. *At Buffalo Mountain Lodge, corner of Tunnel Mountain Dr. and Coyote Dr.* ☎ *403/762-2400. www.crmr.com/buffalo/dining. Entrees $15–$22. AE, MC, V. June 28–Sept 5 Wed–Sun 5–10pm. Closed Sept 6–late June. Map p 68.*

★★ **Coyotes Grill** BANFF *SOUTHWESTERN* Fresh, healthy, relaxed, and very popular with locals, Santa Fe comes to the Rockies here with corn and chile peppers on enchiladas, in soups, and even on pizzas. There's also a superb breakfast. *206 Caribou St.* ☎ *403/762-3963. www.coyotesbanff.com. Entrees $17–$29. AE, MC, V. Daily 7:30am–11pm. Map p 68.*

★ **Eddie Burger and Bar** BANFF *BURGERS* Build your own gourmet burgers well into the evening at this fun and funky bar. The bison burger comes with sautéed mushrooms, double-smoked bacon, and roasted garlic aioli on an English muffin. Add sweet potato fries and a milkshake. *137C Banff Ave. (on Caribou St.).* ☎ *403/762-2230. www.eddieburgerbar.ca. Entrees $8–$16. MC, V. Daily 11:30am–3am. Map p 68.*

★★ **Eden at Rimrock** BANFF *FRENCH* Request table no. 2 at Banff's most luxurious restaurant for views and romance. The refined French-influenced menu ranges from three- to eight-course tastings at Western Canada's only 5-diamond CAA/AAA award winner. *Rimrock Resort Hotel, 300 Mountain Ave.* ☎ *403/762-1840. www.rimrockresort.com. Tasting menus $100–$300. AE, DC, MC, V. Daily 6–10pm. Map p 68.*

★ **Elk & Oarsmen** BANFF *PUB* Settle in with some locals to watch the game and dig into the best pub food in Banff. Recommended choices are the Black Angus steaks or a burger (you have elk, bison, beef, salmon, or chorizo to choose from!). There's a great patio on the rooftop, regular happy-hour specials, and big-screen TVs. *119 Banff Ave., second floor.* ☎ *403/762-4616. www.elkandoarsman.com. Entrees $14–$32. AE, MC, V. Daily 11am–11pm (pub stays open later). Map p 68.*

Evelyn's BANFF *COFFEE SHOP* Where Banff locals head for a coffee. Evelyn's now has three locations around town; the two Banff Avenue locations often have long lineups of tourists looking for caffeine. Quieter is the shop beneath the movie theater, known as Evelyn's Too. Lunch items include thick fresh sandwiches and daily soup specials. *229 Bear St.* ☎ *403/762-0330. www.evelynscoffeebar.com. Entrees $8–$12. MC, V. Daily 7am–6pm. Map p 68.*

★ Giorgio's Trattoria BANFF
ITALIAN Since a new chef took over, Giorgio's is more relaxed, fresh, and simple. Dine Italian family-style by sharing dishes like an antipasto platter, risotto, and a wood-fired pizza. Don't want to share? Then you can't miss the Tuscan Caesar salad and veal scaloppini. *219 Banff Ave.* ☎ *403/762-5114. www.giorgiosbanff.com. Entrees $16–$33. AE, MC, V. Daily 5–10pm. Map p 68.*

Grizzly House BANFF *FONDUE*
Fondue has never gone out of style at this over-the-top alcove on Banff Avenue. Veggie, chicken, prawn, beef, even buffalo can get dropped into the pot. There's plenty of retro-shtick here to temper the steaming pots of fondue and the smoking hot plates. Things can get rowdy and noisy in here, though. *207 Banff Ave.* ☎ *403/762-4055. www.banff grizzlyhouse.com. Entrees $17–$48. AE, MC, V. Daily 11:30am–midnight. Map p 68.*

Juniper Bistro BANFF *CANA-DIAN*
Just out of town, the main draw to this bistro is its sunny patio,

one of the nicest in town. The menu has hearty pub food, like dark ale bison ribs and a fish hot pot. *Bottom of Mt. Norquay Rd. in the Juniper Hotel.* ☎ *403/763-6205. www.the juniper.com. Entrees $18–$34. AE, MC, V. Daily 7:30am–9:30pm. Map p 68.*

The Keg at Caribou Lodge
BANFF *STEAKHOUSE* They've got everything from filet mignons to rib steaks, but the stars here are grilled sirloins and prime rib. There are two Keg locations in Banff, both along Banff Avenue. But the one inside the Caribou Lodge has a cozy, wooden-framed atmosphere, great service, and consistently top-notch steaks. They are also open for breakfast. *521 Banff Ave.* ☎ *403/762-4442. www. kegsteakhouse.com. Entrees $21–$38. AE, MC, V. Daily 6:30am–midnight.*

Le Beaujolais BANFF
FRENCH Banff's long-standing fine dining establishment has fancy and good French food, but the atmosphere doesn't live up to the food or the prices. A few standouts include the Quebec foie gras ravioli or the very traditional Chateaubriand-style entrecote. There is a more casual bistro next door, Café de Paris, run out of the same kitchen. *Corner of Buffalo and Banff sts.* ☎ *403/762-5365. www.lebeaujolaisbanff.com.*

The Caribou Room at Maple Leaf Grille.

Nourish has excellent vegetarian options.

Entrees $22–$40. AE, MC, V. Daily 5–10pm; Sat–Sun noon–4pm. Map p 68.

★★ Maple Leaf Grill BANFF *CANADIAN* Canadian classics such as rainbow trout and venison vie with Alberta bison and Atlantic salmon beneath a birchbark canoe in a room that feels more like a lodge. Although casual in atmosphere, the food is decidedly upscale. There's an award-winning wine list with over 100 Canadian labels. *137 Banff Ave.* ☎ *403/760-7680. www.banffmapleleaf.com. Entrees $22–$48. AE, DISC, MC, V. Daily 10am–2am. Map p 68.*

Nourish BANFF *VEGETARIAN* If you're tired of steaks and gamey meat, this friendly second-floor restaurant in the Sundance Mall has organic, vegan, wheat-free, and gluten-free choices. Even non-vegetarians will like the nacho platter or wild-mushroom ravioli with lavender sauce. The decor is funky and colorful. *215 Banff Ave.* ☎ *403/760-3933. www.nourishbistro.com. Entrees $16–$27. AE, MC, V. Wed–Mon noon–3pm and 5–9pm. Map p 68.*

kids Old Spaghetti Factory BANFF *ITALIAN* Expect no-frills Italian specialties like lasagna and pesto linguini. Entrees all include soup or salad, garlic bread, and an ice-cream dessert. There are always great specials and bargains here, especially for families. *Cascade Plaza, 317 Banff Ave., second floor.* ☎ *403/760-2779. www.oldspaghetti factory.ca. Entrees $10–$16. AE, MC, V. Daily 11:30am–10pm. Map p 68.*

★ kids Phil's BANFF *CANADIAN* Nothing is fancy at Phil's. Think spaghetti with meatballs, a chicken breast with gravy and mashed potatoes, or beef liver with bacon and onions. Breakfast portions are massive. With free baby food, crayons, lots of booster seats, and an excellent kids' menu, families can't find a better spot. *109 Spray Ave.* ☎ *403/762-2902. Entrees $9–$17. AE, MC, V. Daily 6:30am–8pm. Map p 68.*

★★★ Post Hotel LAKE LOUISE *REGIONAL* Blending fine dining with a rustic elegance, the Swiss chef uses European techniques and regional ingredients, mainly meats like veal tenderloin, caribou striploin, and rack of lamb. Service is first-class. The real star, though, is a massive wine cellar. *200 Pipestone.* ☎ *403/522-2167. www.posthotel. com. Entrees $32–$52. AE, MC, V. Daily 11:30am–2pm and 6–10pm. Map p 68.*

★★ Saltlik BANFF *STEAKHOUSE*
With a modern, trendy twist, steaks here are fast-cooked in a 1,200°F (649°C) infrared oven. Top it with a marinade like chipotle barbecue or citrus rosemary. A lounge downstairs features live jazz and martinis. *221 Bear St. ☎ 403/762-2467. www. saltlik.com. Entrees $19–$44. AE, MC, V. Daily noon–1am. Map p 68.*

★ Sleeping Buffalo BANFF *REGIONAL* One of the earliest promoters of Rocky Mountain cuisine, there is an impressive selection of very local meats here. The sample platter has smoked buffalo, venison ham, and elk salami. An incredibly tender bison rib-eye stands out in the entrees list. *700 Tunnel Mountain Rd. at the Buffalo Mountain Lodge. ☎ 403/760-4484. www. crmr.com/buffalo/dining. AE, MC, V. Entrees $26–$38. Daily noon–10pm. Map p 68.*

Sukiyaki House BANFF *JAPANESE* The best traditional Japanese food in Banff. The Love Boat—a wooden board filled with a wide variety of sushi, including sashimi and maki, plus vegetable tempura—easily feeds two hungry hikers and comes with miso soup and rice. *211 Banff*

Trendy Saltlik is known for its steaks.

Wild Flour Bakery is popular throughout the day.

Ave., second floor, Park Avenue Mall. ☎ 403/762-2002. www.sukiyaki house.com. Entrees $14–$34. AE, MC, V. Daily 4:30–10pm. Map p 68.

Wild Flour Bakery and Café BANFF *CAFE* Bustling from dawn to dusk, this is Banff's best bakery and a great spot for lunch. Their sandwiches are excellent—try the pulled pork with apple barbecue sauce or the gourmet grilled cheese. There's always a soup and focaccia of the day. Grab a protein bar for an afternoon snack. *221 Bear St. ☎ 403/760-5074. www.wildflour bakery.ca. Entrees $7–$10. AE, MC, V. Mon–Thurs 7am–6pm; Fri–Sat 7am–6pm.*

Lodging in **Banff National Park**

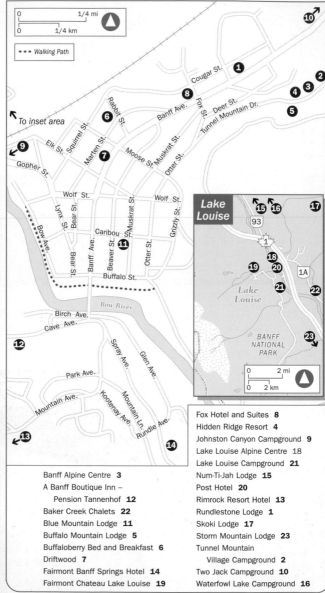

Fox Hotel and Suites **8**
Hidden Ridge Resort **4**
Johnston Canyon Campground **9**
Lake Louise Alpine Centre **18**
Lake Louise Campground **21**
Num-Ti-Jah Lodge **15**
Post Hotel **20**
Rimrock Resort Hotel **13**
Rundlestone Lodge **1**
Skoki Lodge **17**
Storm Mountain Lodge **23**
Tunnel Mountain
   Village Campground **2**
Two Jack Campground **10**
Waterfowl Lake Campground **16**

Banff Alpine Centre **3**
A Banff Boutique Inn –
   Pension Tannenhof **12**
Baker Creek Chalets **22**
Blue Mountain Lodge **11**
Buffalo Mountain Lodge **5**
Buffaloberry Bed and Breakfast **6**
Driftwood **7**
Fairmont Banff Springs Hotel **14**
Fairmont Chateau Lake Louise **19**

Lodging Best Bets

Best Backcountry
★★ Skoki Lodge $$ *In Banff National Park; access from trail head at Temple Lodge next to Lake Louise Ski Resort (p 82)*

Best Boutique Hotel
★ A Banff Boutique Inn—Pension Tannenhof $$ *121 Cave Ave. (p 78)*

Best on a Budget
★ Blue Mountain Lodge $ *327 Caribou St. (p 79)*

Best for Business
Rimrock Resort Hotel $$$ *300 Mountain Ave. (p 81)*

Best Historic Charm
★★ Post Hotel $$$ *200 Pipestone (p 81)*

Best for Families
Fox Hotel and Suites $$ *46 Banff Ave. (p 80)*

Best for Meeting Hiking Partners
Banff Alpine Centre $ *801 Hidden Ridge Way (p 78)*

Best Local Knowledge
★ A Banff Boutique Inn—Pension Tannenhof $$ *121 Cave Ave. (p 78)*

Best Night's Sleep
Buffaloberry Bed and Breakfast $$ *417 Marten St. (p 79)*

Best Scenery
Num-Ti-Jah Lodge $$ *Icefields Pkwy. (p 81)*

Best Spa
★★ Willow Stream at the Fairmont Banff Springs $$$ *405 Spray Ave. (p 79)*

Best View
★★ Fairmont Chateau Lake Louise $$$ *111 Lake Louise Dr. (p 80)*

Best for Wildlife Watching
★ Baker Creek Chalets $$ *11km (6¾ miles) southeast of Lake Louise and 14km (8¾ miles) north of Castle Junction on the Bow Valley Pkwy., Hwy. 1A. (p 78)*

The scenery at Num-Ti-Jah Lodge is hard to beat.

Lodging A to Z

Travel Tip

All prices given are for summer rates, which are in effect from about June 15 to September 15. If you travel outside this peak season—except for around the Christmas holidays—rates should be lower. Check the hotels' websites for packages and deals.

★ **kids Baker Creek Chalets**
LAKE LOUISE   In a semisecluded spot just south of Lake Louise, this collection of red-roofed cabins and lodges is really amid the wild—bears, elk, and deer routinely stroll by. Cabins mainly sleep four to six and have kitchenettes. It's the kind of place you want to settle in and spend an entire week, well worth at least a night or two away from busy Banff. The train runs sporadically throughout the day and night next to the property; if you are a light sleeper, ask for their quietest cabins. *11km (6¾ miles) southeast of Lake Louise and 14km (8¾ miles) north of Castle Junction on the Bow Valley Pkwy., Hwy. 1A.* ☎ *403/522-2270. www.bakercreek.com.*

Inside a cabin at Baker Creek Chalets.

35 units. Doubles $285–$405. AE, MC, V. Map p 76.

Banff Alpine Centre BANFF   Fun and reasonably priced, this hostel is just outside the Banff Townsite on Tunnel Mountain Road. Dorm rooms sleep four to six people, and there are five double rooms with private bathrooms that are a good bargain. The pub is always lively. *801 Hidden Ridge Way.* ☎ *403/762-4123. www.hihostels.ca/alberta. 52 units, which accommodate btw. 2 and 6 people, or 216 beds. Beds from $37; private doubles from $123. MC, V. Map p 76.*

★ **A Banff Boutique Inn—Pension Tannenhof** BANFF   A local couple with a passion for inn-keeping has turned an old-fashioned building into a lovely inn, with modern decor and mountain hospitality. It's a breath of fresh air in Banff. Rooms have strange layouts, some with very small bathrooms, but the vibe is relaxing and breakfasts superb. *121 Cave Ave.* ☎ *403/762-4636. www.banffboutiqueinn.com. 10 units. Doubles $175–$310. Breakfast included. MC, V. Map p 76.*

The Fairmont Banff Springs Hotel is one of the most famous buildings in Canada.

★ **Blue Mountain Lodge** BANFF
Offering simple, clean, and pleasant rooms, the owners at this little place go the extra mile, from a superb breakfast to afternoon home-baked snacks and free wireless. Just steps from Banff Avenue, this is a good choice for people with limited budgets who want to be close to the action. *327 Caribou St.* ☎ *403/762-5134. www.bluemtnlodge.com. 10 units. Doubles $119–$179. MC, V. Map p 76.*

Buffalo Mountain Lodge BANFF
With peeled log frames, feather duvets over flannel sheets, fieldstone fireplaces, and log furniture, there's a preppy cottage feel to this collection of buildings on Tunnel Mountain. It's one of the more classy places in town, but maintains a casually elegant, outdoorsy feel. *700 Tunnel Mountain Rd.* ☎ *800/661-1367 or 403/762-2400. www.crmr.com. 108 units. Doubles $259–$349. AE, MC, V. Map p 76.*

Buffaloberry Bed and Breakfast BANFF   The unpretentious owners of this little inn love the outdoors, and their B&B, in a building nestled in one of downtown Banff's quieter areas, may be the best sleep in town, thanks to soundproof rooms, blackout curtains, solid-core doors, and luxurious natural linens. Bathrooms are spacious. *417 Marten St.* ☎ *403/762-3750. www.buffaloberry.com. 4 units. Doubles*

$335. Breakfast included. MC, V. Map p 76.

Driftwood BANFF   If all you really want is a comfortable and clean place to sleep after spending the days in the great mountains, this is an undiscovered gem. Since it's next door to the Ptarmigan Inn, and has the same owners, guests have use of the restaurant, hot tub, and wireless at bargain prices. The beds are super soft and topped with fluffy duvets. *337 Banff Ave.* ☎ *800/661-8310 or 403/762-4496. www.bestofbanff.com/tdi. 32 units. Doubles $129–169. AE, DISC, MC, V. Map p 76.*

★★ **Fairmont Banff Springs Hotel** BANFF   One of the most famous buildings in Canada, this spectacular hotel is a true experience. Rooms are notoriously small, so don't plan to spend much time indoors. The Gold Floor has by far the nicest rooms. The list of amenities, from the Willow Stream Spa, to a bowling center, horse stables, and nine restaurants, overwhelms. This is an unforgettable place to spend a few nights, but it doesn't come cheap. Packages including breakfast and online specials will help with the high price tag. *405 Spray Ave.* ☎ *800/441-1414 or 403/762-2211. www.fairmont.com/banffsprings. 768 units. Doubles $449–659. AE, DC, DISC, MC, V. Map p 76.*

A room with a view of the lake at Fairmont Chateau Lake Louise.

★★ Fairmont Chateau Lake Louise LAKE LOUISE
The award-winning landmark hotel is elegant, with a Swiss Alpine feel, and more comfortable than the Banff Springs. Rooms with lake views are much more than those on the other side of the hall (which still have nice mountain views). The Gold Floor offers superior service. The pool is nothing special, but the hotel's rich heritage, coupled with access to amazing hiking and skiing, is unmatched on the planet. *111 Lake Louise Dr.* ☎ *800/441-1414 or 403/522-3511. www.fairmont.com/lakelouise. 554 units. Doubles $349–$499. AE, DISC, DC, MC, V. Map p 76.*

kids Fox Hotel and Suites BANFF
More contemporary than most of the hotels in town, rooms are mostly suites with kitchenettes and one or two bedrooms. Loft-style second-floor units have mountain views. The courtyard has a stunning hot pool themed after the historic Banff springs. *46 Banff Ave.* ☎ *800/661-8310 or 403/760-8500. www.bestofbanff.com/fox. 117 units. Doubles $219–$449. AE, DISC, MC, V. Map p 76.*

Hidden Ridge Resort BANFF
If you'd like lots of personal space, and to be away from the bustle of Banff Avenue, this collection of stylish cabins along Tunnel Mountain Road provides privacy in town house–style apartments. In 2009, they added full kitchens and wood-burning fireplaces to all units, and two new outdoor hot pools with fabulous views above Banff. *901 Hidden Ridge Way.* ☎ *800/661-1372 or 403/762-3544. www.bestofbanff.com/hrr. 107 units. Chalets $199–$469. AE, DISC, MC, V. Map p 76.*

Johnston Canyon Campground
This is a tranquil campground nestled in a pleasant forest less than 20 minutes from Banff Townsite. The nicest of the sites back onto Johnston Creek. *25km (16 miles) west of Banff Townsite on the Bow Valley Pkwy., Hwy. 1A. No reservations. 132 sites. No RV hookups. Sites $27. AE, MC, V. Closed Sept 15–May 28. Map p 76.*

Lake Louise Alpine Centre LAKE LOUISE
Don't let the fact that this is a hostel turn you off a great value. Rooms range from small dormitories and simple doubles to larger rooms that sleep up to six. Simple communal bathrooms and showers are down the hall. *203 Village Rd.* ☎ *403/522-2201. www.hostellingintl.ca/alberta. 45 units. Dorms from $38. Private rooms from $120. MC, V. Map p 76.*

Lake Louise Campground LAKE LOUISE
This campground is downhill

from the Fairmont Chateau Lake Louise, away from the lake. The tent area is in the trees near the river. The trailer area is more open and closer to the highway and railway line. It's a 10-minute walk to Lake Louise Village. *58km (36 miles) northwest of Banff Townsite on the Trans-Canada Hwy. 1. Exit at Lake Louise and turn left after passing under the railway bridge onto Fairview Rd. Reservations at www. pccamping.ca.* ☎ *877/737-3783. Lake Louise Tent: 206 sites. No RV hookups. $28. Closed Sept 30–May 25. Lake Louise Trailer: 189 sites. Electrical hookups only. $32. Open year-round. Map p 76.*

Num-Ti-Jah Lodge ICEFIELDS

PARKWAY Banff's most scenic lodge is rustic, historic, and secluded. You'll pay for the location, and the expensive dining room (which is the only option), not the amenities. The stairs creak as you climb them and the walls are thin. Rooms are clean, though quite basic. Heaps of character and history manage to cover up the need for a major upgrade. *40km (25 miles) north of Lake Louise on the Icefields Pkwy.* ☎ *403/522-2167. www.num-ti-jah.com. 25 units. Doubles $275–$320. AE, MC, V. Map p 76.*

★★ Post Hotel LAKE LOUISE A

quintessential and exquisite mountain

A common area inside the Lake Louise Alpine Centre.

inn, the Post Hotel combines beautiful guest rooms and excellent service in a peaceful location. Guest rooms are simple but luxurious, with fireplaces, down quilts, and heated slate floors in the bathrooms. The Temple Mountain Spa is the best in Lake Louise. *200 Pipestone.* ☎ *800/661-1586 or 403/522-3989. www.posthotel.com. 92 units. Doubles $345–$850. AE, MC, V. Map p 76.*

Rimrock Resort Hotel BANFF

Modern and slick, the Rimrock has a great view and fine lodgings. The lobby is graced by a giant marble fireplace, cherry oak walls, leather chairs, and big windows offering

A bedroom inside the Fox Hotel and Suites.

A peaceful sitting room at the Post Hotel.

views you can't get even in the penthouses of other local hotels. Peaceful and elegant, rooms are airy, luxurious, and large. Request one on the east face of the south wing for the choicest views. *300 Mountain Ave.* ☎ *800/661-1587 or 403/762-3356. www.rimrockresort. com. 346 units. Doubles $238–$630. AE, DISC, MC, V. Map p 76.*

Rundlestone Lodge BANFF There is a long line of midsize hotels and motels along Banff Avenue. This one stands out for recent renovations that have given it a more modern feel. The gym, pool, and the large size of standard rooms add value. Predictable but clean, the service here is also very friendly. *537 Banff Ave.* ☎ *800/661-8630 or 403/762-2201. www.rundlestone. com. 96 rooms. Doubles $164–$294. AE, DISC, MC, V. Map p 76.*

★★ Skoki Lodge BACKCOUN-TRY This is a classic backcountry lodge built nearly a century ago, so you must ski or hike 11km (6.8 miles) to get here, arriving to a gorgeous valley behind the Lake Louise ski area. The lodge is rustic; there is no electricity or running water. There are, however, incredible trails at your doorstep and true Rocky Mountain seclusion. *Banff National Park.* ☎ *800/258-7669. www.skoki lodge.com. Sleeps up to 22 guests. From $160 per person including meals. AE, MC, V. Map p 76.*

Storm Mountain Lodge BANFF OUTSKIRTS A collection of old-fashioned cabins halfway between Banff and Lake Louise have been nicely restored with large tubs, crackling fireplaces, and comfy beds. Unit nos. 9 and 10 are farthest from the sometimes-noisy Hwy. 93.

Big windows are a feature of rooms at the Rimrock Resort Hotel.

A campsite at Two Jack Campground.

Nos. 11 and 14 have great views of Castle Mountain. *On Hwy. 93 just west of Castle Junction.* ☎ *403/762-4155. www.stormmountainlodge. com. 14 units. Cabins $169–$239. MC, V. Map p 76.*

Travel Tip

Remember that sites at Lake Louise (tent and trailer) and at all Tunnel Mountain campgrounds should be reserved in advance at www.pc camping.ca. All other sites are on a first-come, first-served basis.

Tunnel Mountain Village Campground BANFF

You can walk to Banff Avenue from the park's biggest campground. It's divided into three sections: a mixed tent and RV camp 2.5km (1½ miles) east of town; an RV mecca 4km (2½ miles) east of town; and a trailer- and tenter-friendly section to the east of the RV area. *4km (2½ miles) east of Banff Townsite on Tunnel Mountain Rd. Reservations at www. pccamping.ca.* ☎ *877/737-3783. Tunnel Mountain Village I: 618 sites. No RV hookups. $27. Closed Oct. 2– May 7. Tunnel Mountain Village II: 188 sites. Electrical hookups only. $32. AE, MC, V. Open year-round. Tunnel Mountain Trailer Court: 321 sites. Full hookups. $38. Closed Oct 2–May 7. AE, MC, V. Map p 76.*

Two Jack Campground MINNE-WANKA LOOP

There are two areas here. The main area (which is larger and busier) is just off the road in a densely wooded forest 13km (8 miles) northeast of Banff Townsite, on the Minnewanka Loop. It's quite private, although there are no great views. The second area is next to the lake and is very popular since it is the most scenic and peaceful campground near the Town of Banff. *12km (7½ miles) from Banff Townsite on Minnewanka Loop Rd. Reservations at www.pccamping.ca.* ☎ *877/737-3783. Two Jack Main: 380 sites. RV-friendly but no RV hookups. $22. Closed Sept 9–May 4. Two Jack Lakeside: 74 sites. No RV hookups. $27. Closed Sept 15–May 14. AE, MC, V. Map p 76.*

Waterfowl Lake Campground ICEFIELDS PARKWAY

This is my favorite in the park because of the scenery and peacefulness. There is an open area on the lakeshore for relaxing or playing games, plus amazing views of the surrounding mountains and glaciers. *57km (35 miles) north of Lake Louise on the Icefields Pkwy., Hwy. 93. No reserva- tions. 116 sites. No RV hookups. $22. Closed Sept 8–June 18. No credit cards. Map p 76.*

Banff **Shopping, Arts & Nightlife**

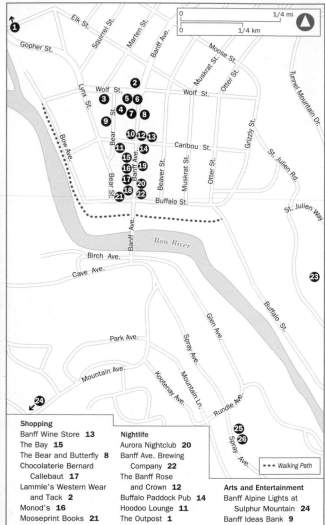

Shopping

Banff Wine Store **13**
The Bay **15**
The Bear and Butterfly **8**
Chocolaterie Bernard
    Callebaut **17**
Lammle's Western Wear
    and Tack **2**
Monod's **16**
Mooseprint Books **21**
Moountain Magic
    Equipment **4**
Philippe of Banff **18**
Qiviuk **26**
Roots **6**

Nightlife

Aurora Nightclub **20**
Banff Ave. Brewing
    Company **22**
The Banff Rose
    and Crown **12**
Buffalo Paddock Pub **14**
Hoodoo Lounge **11**
The Outpost **1**
Saint James's Gate **5**
Tommy's Neighbourhood
    Pub **19**
Wild Bill's Legendary
    Saloon **10**

••• *Walking Path*

Arts and Entertainment

Banff Alpine Lights at
    Sulphur Mountain **24**
Banff Ideas Bank **9**
The Banff Centre **23**
Bowling at Fairmont
    Banff Springs **25**
Evening Wildlife Safari **7**
Lux Theatre **3**

Shopping & Nightlife
Best Bets

Best for **Backcountry Gear**
Mountain Magic Equipment, *224 Bear St. (p 87)*

Best **Cowboy Culture**
Wild Bill's, *201 Banff Ave. (p 90);* and Lammle's Cascade Plaza, *317 Banff Ave. (p 87)*

Best **Dance Floor**
Aurora Nightclub, *110 Banff Ave. (p 89)*

Best **Family Night Out**
Lux Theatre, *229 Bear St. (p 89)*

Best **Outdoor Fashion**
Monod's, *129 Banff Ave. (p 87)*

Best **for Singles**
Hoodoo Lounge, *137 Banff Ave. (p 90)*

Best **Jazz**
The Banff Centre, *107 Tunnel Mountain Rd. (p 88)*

Best **Low-Key Après Ski**
Tommy's Neighbourhood Pub, *120 Banff Ave. (p 90)*

Best **Selection of Beer on Tap**
★ Saint James's Gate, *205 Wolf St. (p 90)*

Cowboy hats at Lammle's Western Wear and Tack.

Shopping, Arts & Nightlife
A to Z

Shopping

Banff Tea Company BANFF
With more than 180 teas from around the world, from oolong to souchong, you're sure to find something to keep your Thermos tasty while you're out exploring the Rockies. The Rocky Mountain Blend has two kinds of black teas and some Rooibos. Brought to you by the same folks that run the Plain of the Six Glaciers Teahouse (p 146), a portion of proceeds are donated to local charities. *208 Caribou St.* ☎ *403/762-8322. www.banffteaco. com. AE, MC, V.*

Banff Wine Store BANFF   The staff at this basement-level shop is incredibly knowledgeable and friendly. Ask for tips on a post-hike pinot or an après-ski cabernet. There are labels from more than a dozen countries and a wide price range, including Canadian ice wine. They also deliver to your hotel! *302 Caribou St.* ☎ *403/782-3465. AE, MC, V. Map p 84.*

The Bay BANFF   The Hudson's Bay Company is a Canadian institution established in 1670. Today, the Bay sells everything from cosmetics to Cuisinarts in their three-level department store. Souvenirs here include maple candies, the famous Hudson's Bay blankets, and Olympic uniforms. *125 Banff Ave.* ☎ *403/762-5525. www.hbc.com. AE, DC, DISC, MC, V. Map p 84.*

Chocolaterie Bernard Callebaut BANFF   This Belgian-born Calgarian is a fifth-generation chocolate maker who says he eats at least six different chocolates each day. His Banff store, inside the Harmony Lane mall, is practically an education in all things chocolate. Choose from 48 flavors, including dark chocolate–coated ginger, ganache cream, and truffles. *111 Banff Ave.* ☎ *403/762-4106. www. bernardcallebaut.com. AE, MC, V. Map p 84.*

Lammle's Western Wear and Tack BANFF   For true-blue cowboy gear, head upstairs in Cascade Plaza. Start with a Shady Brady cowboy hat and a pair of Wrangler jeans with a silver belt; then wrap up the

Some of the delectables for sale at Chocolaterie Bernard Callebaut.

Seashell
hazelnut paste

Manon
marzipan, walnut, meringue

Souvenirs on display at the Bay.

whole outfit with a pair of Dan Post cowboy boots. They also have kid-swear for junior saddle ropers. *Cascade Plaza, 317 Banff Ave.* ☎ *403/762-5460. www.lammles. com. AE, MC, V. Map p 84.*

Monod's BANFF   Banff's oldest outdoor clothing and equipment retailer is a busy, jampacked shop staffed by keen outdoorsy types. Hiking boots are upstairs at the back, along with fly-fishing rods, while climbing harnesses and tents are downstairs, and cold-weather wear right in the middle. Fleeces, puffy vests, or zip-off pants, anyone? *129 Banff Ave.* ☎ *403/762-4571. www.monodsports.com. AE, MC, V. Map p 84.*

Mooseprint Books BANFF   The newest bookstore in town is across from Central Park and has just about every book ever published about the Rockies—from kids' coloring books to hiking guides and wild-flower pocketbooks. They also have unique souvenirs, gorgeous coffee-table books, and a handful of recent best-selling paperbacks. *208 Buffalo St.* ☎ *403/762-3355. www.moose print.com. AE, MC, V. Map p 84.*

Mountain Magic Equipment BANFF   For backpacking, climbing, mountaineering, camping, or any other kind of alpine adventure, this shop is the go-to place for gear-heads. The staff is made up of knowledgeable and friendly moun-tain men and women. And rentals are available for things like tents and avalanche transceivers. *224 Bear St.* ☎ *403/762-2591. www. mountainmagic.com. AE, MC, V. Map p 84.*

Philippe of Banff BANFF   Since Banff is the jewel of the Rockies, it's only appropriate that you'd find some diamonds at this fine jeweler's atelier. Banff goldsmith Philippe Plourde handcrafts stunning jewelry that hon-ors tradition yet embraces modern styles. *130 Banff Ave.* ☎ *403/760-8744. AE, MC, V. Map p 84.*

Qiviuk BANFF   Celebrities have discovered that it's softer than cash-mere, warmer than beaver or fox fur, lighter than wool. The supple and plush pelt from the Canadian Arctic musk ox comes from the Far North, making qiviuk the world's rar-est natural fiber. This store in the Banff Springs sells sweaters, coats, hats, shawls, and scarves. *Fairmont Banff Springs Hotel, 405 Spray Ave.* ☎ *403/762-4460. www.qiviuk.com. AE, DC, MC, V. Map p 84.*

Roots BANFF   Canada's iconic leather and casual clothing shop is a great place for a maple-leaf–inspired souvenir, from hoodies to baby sleepers. They've lately started dabbling in yoga wear and linens, but maintain their—um, roots—with sweats. This is your chance to adapt the Canadian lifestyle with genuine leather and always-stylish purses, jackets, and shoes. *277 Banff Ave.* ☎ *403/762-9434. http://canada. roots.com. AE, MC, V. Map p 84.*

Rude Girls BANFF   Every female shredder or ripper needs the clothes and style to go with the big-mountain attitude. This boutique (the sister of Rude Boys, which shares the store) has edgy, punky fashion for girls who like to snowboard, ski, skateboard, surf, or just generally want to look cool. *203 Caribou St.* ☎ *403/762-8211. www.rudeboys.com. AE, MC, V.*

Arts & Entertainment
Banff Alpine Lights at Sulphur Mountain BANFF   Ride the Sulphur Mountain Gondola on Saturday nights during summertime and combine it with an unforgettable "Prime Rib Prime View" dinner way, way above the lights of town. *At the end of Mountain Rd., 2.5km (1½ miles) from Banff Ave.* ☎ *403/762-2523. www.explorerockies.com. Sat only*

Outerwear for sale at Monod's.

June 13–Oct 10 5–9pm. Adults $49, kids $27. Map p 84.

★★★ The Banff Centre BANFF
For inspiring concerts featuring world-class jazz, dance, pop, folk, and world music, keep an eye on the calendar and hope something is happening during your visit. *St. Julien Rd.* ☎ *403/762-6301. www. banffcentre.ca. Wed and Fri–Sun 9pm–2am. Admission varies. Map p 84.*

Banff Ideas Bank BANFF   If you are lucky enough to be in town for one of these monthly evening events, don't miss it. Locals and visitors gather for "Conversation Cafes" to discuss issues relevant to living in Banff, such as: how to keep youth in town; what does it mean to live in a national park; and how to make the most of life in Banff. Stirring chatter and friendly faces make this a superb chance to soak up the local scene. *Held at the Wild Flour Bakery, 211 Bear St., the first Wednesday of each month at 7pm. www.banff ideasbank.ca.*

kids Bowling at Fairmont Banff Springs BANFF   There are four lanes of five-pin bowling at the Fairmont Banff Springs Hotel, which

Dancers perform at the Banff Centre.

makes for a lively and fun family evening activity, especially on a stormy night. There's also a video game arcade and bar inside. *405 Spray Ave., in the Conference Centre.* ☎ *403/762-6892. www.fairmont. com/banffsprings. Adults $6/game, kids 10 and under $5.50/game. Mon–Thurs 3–10pm; Fri–Sat 10am–11pm; Sun 1–7pm. Map p 84.*

★ Evening Wildlife Safari

BANFF   Two-hour van-based wildlife tours run by Discover Banff Tours depart Banff each evening, taking full advantage of what is perhaps your best bet for wildlife sightings. The guides are very good, and binoculars are provided. *Discover Banff Tours' office is in Sundance Mall, 215 Banff Ave.* ☎ *403/760-5007. www.banfftours.com. Daily at 6:30pm. Adults $40, kids 5–12 $25. Map p 84.*

Lux Theatre BANFF   Banff's venerable cinema plays mainly first-run Hollywood hits, and there's always a family-friendly blockbuster running. *229 Bear St.* ☎ *403/762-8595. www. landmarkcinemas.ca. Adults $10, children 11 and under $7. Map p 84.*

Nightlife

Aurora Nightclub BANFF   The best spot for later-night dancing and funky techno atmosphere. There's a cigar room, a martini bar, and karaoke

on Thursdays. *110 Banff Ave., downstairs.* ☎ *403/760-5300. www.aurora banff.com. Admission varies $6-$12. Map p 84.*

Banff Ave. Brewing Company

BANFF   It's "all about the beer" at this second-story microbrewery, particularly lively in the après-ski, or après-work (yes, people in Banff do work) hours. A sampler lets you try their half-dozen specialties. The menu is staple pub food—try the meatloaf or a huge serving of poutine. *111 Banff Ave., 2nd floor.* ☎ *403/762-1003. www.banffave brewingco.com. Daily 11:30am–2am. Free admission. Map p 84.*

The Banff Rose and Crown

BANFF   With a spacious rooftop patio and a long list of beers on tap, this is a laid-back favorite with a low-brow style. There is often live music, including Maritime Mondays for fans of the East Coast. *202 Banff Ave., upstairs.* ☎ *403/762-2121. www. roseandcrown.ca. Admission varies $4–$12. Daily 11am–2am. Map p 84.*

Buffalo Paddock Pub BANFF

On the top floor of the Mt. Royal Hotel, come for billiards, darts, shuffleboard, foosball, and more than a dozen large-screen TVs. *124 Banff Ave.* ☎ *403/760-8543. www.mount royalhotel.com. Free admission. Daily noon–2am. Map p 84.*

The bar at Aurora Nightclub.

Hoodoo Lounge BANFF Those who really want to party can join the young crowd in the basement here for top-20 dance tunes. Specials practically every night of the week, from ladies' night to live music. *137 Banff Ave.* ☎ *403/760-8636. www. hoodoolounge.com. Admission varies $5–$14. Daily 9pm–2am. Closed Wed and Sun. Map p 84.*

The Outpost LAKE LOUISE The best spot for an evening drink in Lake Louise is in the basement pub beneath the Post Hotel for draft beer and light pub food similar to the gourmet stuff on offer upstairs. *200 Pipestone.* ☎ *403/522-3989. Free admission. Daily 4:30pm– midnight. Map p 84.*

★ **Saint James's Gate** BANFF Inspired by the birthplace of Guinness, selecting a draught here is just about the toughest challenge in Banff—there are 33 beers on tap, as well as 50 single-malt scotches and 10 Irish whiskeys. Live music is almost always Celtic, and a blast. *205 Wolf St.* ☎ *403/762-9355. www. stjamesgatebanff.com. Admission varies, $4–$14. Daily 11am–2am. Map p 84.*

Tommy's Neighbourhood Pub BANFF Locals here are happy to share stories of what it's like to live in such a storied town. This is a friendly place where you can actually have a conversation without yelling. *120 Banff Ave.* ☎ *403/762- 8888. www.tommysneighbourhood pub.com. Free admission. Daily 11am–2am. Map p 84.*

★ **Wild Bill's Legendary Saloon** BANFF The local cowboy hangout is fun and not necessarily all about the yee-haw. What can I say? Head here if you want to drink beer and do some line dancing. Wednesday nights brings line-dance lessons. *201 Banff Ave., upstairs.* ☎ *403/762-0333. www.wbsaloon. com. Admission varies, $5–$18. Daily 11am–2am. Map p 84.* ●

The Canadian Rockies

Kananaskis Country

0 —————— 10 mi	
0 —————— 10 km	

Ghost River Wilderness

Cascade Mtn.

Mt. Norquay

Lake Minnewanka

1A

Banff

BANFF NATIONAL PARK

Mt. Rundle

Park Gate

ALBERTA

To Calgary ↗

1A

Canmore

Exshaw

Seebe

Bow Valley Prov. Park

❶

Spray River

Bow Valley Wildland Provincial Park

Mt. Assiniboine Provincial Park

Spray Lakes Reservoir

Buller Mountain

❷
❸ Kananaskis Village
❹
❺

Spray Valley Provincial Park

Marvel Lake

Mt. Assiniboine

742

Fortress Mountain

40

Elbow-Sheep Wildland Provincial Park

Peter Lougheed Provincial Park

Mt. Sir Douglas

BRITISH COLUMBIA

Kananaskis Lakes

❻

Legend

△ Campground
⛽ Gasoline
✚ Hospital/First Aid
ⓘ Information
◼ Point of Interest
⛷ Ski Resort

❶ Barrier Lake Visitors Centre
❷ Nakiska
❸ Kananaskis Village
❹ Fireweed Grill
❺ Kananaskis Country Golf Course
❻ Peter Lougheed Visitors Centre

Inset map:
Edmonton
ALBERTA
16
40
16
2
Jasper
93
BRITISH COLUMBIA
Lake Louise
Golden
Calgary
Banff
2
Area of map
CANADA
UNITED STATES

Previous Page: Hiking at beautiful Lake O'Hara.

Kananaskis Country is a vast area of rugged mountain wilderness that contains four provincial parks and "multiple-use" land where forestry, cattle-grazing, and petroleum development are permitted. From the golf courses to the trails, things are quiet here compared to Banff, drawing mainly weekenders from Calgary. Kananaskis is named for a Cree native who was reportedly struck by an axe but survived. There's a good variety of outdoor activities, gorgeous scenery, and excellent infrastructure. **START: Banff.**

From Banff, take the Trans-Canada Highway west 55km (34 miles). Turn south on Hwy. 40, the Kananaskis Trail.

❶ Barrier Lake Visitors Centre. This is a good first stop, at the entrance to Kananaskis Country on Hwy. 40. Pick up brochures and maps. 🕐 15 min. Hwy. 40, 8km (5 miles) south of Trans-Canada Hwy. 1. ☎ 403/673-3985. May 12–June 28 Mon–Fri 9:30am–4pm, Sat–Sun 9am–5pm; June 29–Sept 3 Fri 8:30am–6pm, Sat–Thurs 8:30am–5pm; Sept 4 to mid-May daily 9:30am–4pm.

Continue south on Hwy. 40 for 14km (8⅔ miles). Turn right towards Kananaskis Village, continuing straight for 2.5km (1½ miles).

❷ Nakiska. The site of the alpine skiing events at the 1988 Calgary Winter Olympics, this is a great family ski hill, steps from Kananaskis Village on the lower slopes of Mt. Allan. Pop by for a photo op beside

The Kananaskis Country Golf Course.

The chair lift at Nakiska ski resort.

assorted Olympic paraphernalia. *2.5km (1½ miles) from Kananaskis Village on Village Rd.* ☎ *403/591-7777. www.skinakiska.com.*

Return back toward Hwy. 40, turning right after 2.5km (1½ miles).

❸ Kananaskis Village. The heart of "K-Country" is home to a golf course, tennis courts, hotels, horse-riding stables, a cafe, and plenty of trails. It's a year-round resort hub that offers a pleasant stroll and a handful of shops. *26km (16 miles) south of Trans-Canada Hwy. 1 on Hwy. 40. Turn right on Mt. Allen Dr. and left on Centennial Dr. Follow directions to parking lot.*

Mt. Kidd in Peter Lougheed Provincial Park.

Pop into the Delta Lodge at Kananaskis for lunch at the **❹Fireweed Grill**. On a summer day, sit on the patio. There are plenty of pizzas and salads to choose from, but I suggest the indulgent Alberta beef dip, famous in these parts. *1 Centennial Dr., Kananaskis Village.* ☎ *403/591-6272. $$.*

Head north out of the Village and then turn left at the first stop sign.

❺ Kananaskis Country Golf Course. Two 18-hole, par-72 courses make up one of the top-rated and most scenic golf resorts in Canada. *Clubhouse is on Lorette Dr. south of Kananaskis Village.* ☎ *877/591-2525 or 403/591-7272. www.kananaskis golf.com. Greens fees $98. Open 7am–10pm, early May to mid-Oct.*

Continue south on Hwy. 40 for 30km (19 miles), turn west on

Kananaskis Lakes Trail and travel 3.7km (2⅓ miles).

❻ Peter Lougheed Provincial Park. Easy interpretive trails lead out from an excellent visitor center onto the shores of the lovely Upper and Lower Kananaskis Lakes. A more demanding hike goes up from the peninsula in between the two lakes to Mt. Indefatigable for superb valley views (hiking boots a must!). Mountain bikers come for the Pocaterra Trail. ☎ *403/591-6322. June–Sept daily 9am–8pm; Oct–May Mon–Thurs 9:30am–4:30pm, Fri–Sat 9am–5pm.*

Chinook Country

Don't be surprised by quick and drastic rises in temperatures during wintertime here. When warm Pacific air comes funneling through to the foothills and slams into a cold high pressure air mass, dry air is compressed and heated, dropping quickly and producing a phenomenon known as a chinook. Local temperatures can go up as much as 72°F (40°C) in 20 minutes. Most winters bring 20 chinook days a year to the eastern edge of the Canadian Rockies near Kananaskis Country.

Canmore

1. Grassi Lakes
2. Good Earth Coffee Co.
3. Canmore Geoscience Museum
4. Avens Gallery
5. Bow River Walk
6. Harvest
7. Canmore Nordic Centre Provincial Park

••• Walking Path

It's hard to beat Canmore. The town of **12,000 boasts** beautiful scenery, world-class trails, plus a relatively short commute to Banff or Calgary. Mountains rise high in all directions, and the turquoise Bow River flows through town. Locals take pride in healthy living, the great cafes and restaurants, and the keen arts scene that have earned Canmore the nickname of "Alberta's Aspen." Many visitors stay here for hotel rates that are typically lower than in Banff, making it a good place to begin day trips into the park. The best way to explore Canmore is on foot. **START: Downtown Canmore.**

At the west end of Main Street, turn left and drive over the Bow River. Turn left again at Three Sisters Drive and right onto Spray Lakes Road. One kilometer (⅔ mile) past the Nordic Centre, turn left into a parking lot for the trail head.

1 ★★ Grassi Lakes. Start the day with a moderate, short, but stunning hike just above town. It's a 4km (2.5-mile) loop that takes you up historic steps, past a waterfall, and on to two small, jewel-like lakes. *Just past Nordic Centre on the Smith Dorrien-Spray Lakes Rd.*

Head back down the hill, around the shore of the reservoir, and into town. Park in the lot behind 8th Street and between the library and Information Centre.

A display at the Canmore Geoscience Museum.

2 Good Earth Coffee Co.
Reward yourself with breakfast on Main Street. There are many places to choose from, but the baked goods and deluxe breakfast sandwiches (and the sunny patio) at this new favorite are real standouts. *718 Main St.* ☎ *403/675-1204. Daily 7am–9pm. $.*

In front, across 7th Avenue and just to the left of you is:

3 Canmore Geoscience Museum. From coal mining to Olympic fame, there's human as well as geological history to discover in this museum, housed in Canmore's new Civic Centre, which has won awards for its eco-friendly design. *902b 7th Ave.* ☎ *403/678-2462. www.cmags.org. Admission $5 adults, $3 students and seniors.*

Summer Mon–Tues noon–5pm, Wed–Sun 10am–5pm; Early Sept to mid-May Mon–Fri noon–5pm, Sat–Sun 11am–5pm.

Stroll to the left along Main Street for window shopping. On the south side is the:

4 Avens Gallery. For 20 years, this has been the premier art gallery in Canmore. There's small art (jewelry, sculpture, blown glass), but the most impressive are the large canvases representing the inspiring local scenery. *104–709 Main St.* ☎ *403/678-4471. Wed–Sun 11am–5pm.*

Continue down Main Street and keep straight as Main Street becomes Riverview Place. At the far end of the cul-de-sac, a sign marks the beginning of a walking trail.

Walkers cross a bridge over the Bow River.

5 Bow River Walk. At the end of Main Street, follow footpath signs to the Bow River Walk, which traces both sides of this turquoise alpine river while taking in dazzling mountain scenery. A gentle 30-minute loop takes you over the old railway bridge, past the TransAlta Plant, and back to town over Bridge Road.

Return to Main Street, turning left on 7th Avenue and right on 10th Street.

A skier at the Canmore Nordic Centre.

6 ★ Harvest. This is where locals grab a healthy lunch. Most sandwiches are grilled, croque monsieur style. On Sundays, there are homemade cinnamon buns. It's just off Main Street. *718 10th St. ☎ 403/678-3747. Daily 8:30am–3pm. $.*

Get back in the car and retrace your route up towards Grassi Lakes. Take a right at the large signs.

7 Canmore Nordic Centre Provincial Park. The park was the host of the Nordic skiing and biathlon events for the 1988 Calgary Winter Olympics, and is the only Canadian stop on the Nordic World Cup tour. There are more than 65km (40 miles) of ski trails in winter, 100km (62 miles) of mountain-bike trails in summer, and a Frisbee golf course. *1.8km/1 mile south of Canmore, take Rundle Dr. across the Bow River Bridge; go left at Three Sisters Dr. and right at Spray Lakes Rd.; follow signs. ☎ 403/678-2400.*

Extreme Golf in the Rockies

There are three outstanding golf courses at Canmore. The oldest course in town is the friendly 18-hole **Canmore Golf and Curling Club** (2000 8th Ave.; ☎ 403/678-4785; www.canmoregolf.net), close to downtown, along the Bow River. Greens fees are $80 per person. The clubhouse has one of the best patios in town. On the north side of Canmore is **SilverTip Resort** (1000 SilverTip Trail, exit at the main Canmore exit and take first left before the lights; ☎ 877/877-5444 or 403/678-1600; www.silvertipresort.com). Calling what it offers "extreme mountain golf," this Les Furber–designed 18-hole, par-72 course is one of a kind. Greens fees range from $125 to $175. **Stewart Creek Golf Course** (1 Stewart Creek Rd., via the Three Sisters Pkwy. exit just east of Canmore; ☎ 877/993-4653 or 403/609-6099; www.stewartcreekgolf.com) is another "high mountain" course that winds along the picturesque lower slopes of the Three Sisters Mountain on the south side of the Bow Valley. Greens fees range from $129 to $195.

Icefields Parkway (Jasper)

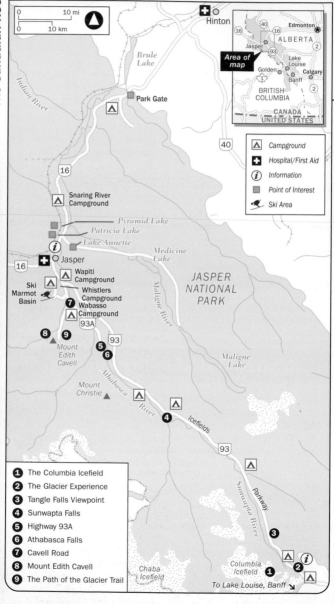

Brule Lake

Hinton

Edmonton
ALBERTA

Jasper
Lake Louise
Calgary
Golden
BRITISH COLUMBIA
Banff

CANADA
UNITED STATES

Area of map

Indian River

Park Gate

40

Campground
Hospital/First Aid
Information
Point of Interest
Ski Area

Snaring River Campground

Pyramid Lake
Patricia Lake
Lake Annette

Medicine Lake

Jasper

JASPER NATIONAL PARK

Wapiti Campground

Ski Marmot Basin

Whistlers Campground
Wabasso Campground

93A

Maligne River

Maligne Lake

Mount Edith Cavell

Mount Christie

Athabasca River

Icefields

93

Sunwapta River

Parkway

Chaba Icefield

Columbia Icefield

To Lake Louise, Banff

1. The Columbia Icefield
2. The Glacier Experience
3. Tangle Falls Viewpoint
4. Sunwapta Falls
5. Highway 93A
6. Athabasca Falls
7. Cavell Road
8. Mount Edith Cavell
9. The Path of the Glacier Trail

As you drive north on the Icefields Parkway, Hwy. 93, you enter Jasper National Park, the largest of the national parks in the Canadian Rockies at 10,878 sq. km (4,200 sq. miles). Large carnivores roam the wide valleys here, so drive slowly and keep an eye out for wildlife; the scenery sometimes more closely resembles the moon than the Rocky Mountains. This tour only covers the highway north of the Icefields Centre; for information on the southern half of the Parkway, see p 64. START: **Icefields Centre, 125km (78 miles) north of Lake Louise and 105km (65 miles) south of Jasper Townsite.**

❶ ★★★ The Columbia Icefield.
The geographical heart of the Icefields Parkway is a world-class natural wonder and living laboratory that examines glaciology and mountain geology. It's fantastically visitor friendly and is located just north of the Banff National Park border, some 103km (64 miles) south of the Town of Jasper. There is a Parks Canada Information Centre inside the Icefields Centre that is open May through late September only, while the building itself is open early April through mid-October. ☎ *780/852-6288.*

❷ ★★ The Glacier Experience.
The venerable Brewster family operates giant "snocoaches" that take you right on to the Athabasca Glacier, giving you a sense of the enormity of this icefield. You get about 15 minutes to walk on top of the 300m–thick (984-ft.) sheets of ice. Although coaches leave every 15 minutes, the tours can be very busy, especially in summer, so reservations are highly recommended. ☎ *403/ 762-6735. www.explorerockies.com.*

Adults $50, kids 6–15 $25, free for kids 5 and under. Apr 6–30 and Oct 1–18 10am–4pm; May 1–31 and Sept 1–30 9am–5pm; June 1–Aug 31 9am–6pm.

Drive north on the Icefields Parkway for 9km (5½ miles).

❸ ★ Tangle Falls Viewpoint.
Just off the west side of the highway at the top of a broad turn are views of the Stutfield Glacier. This is also one of the best chances in the Canadian Rockies to see mountain goats close up, who are drawn to mineral licks on both sides of the road. *96km (60 miles) from Jasper and 9km (5½ miles) from the Icefields Centre. Map p 98.*

Continue north on the Icefields Parkway for 41km (25 miles).

❹ Sunwapta Falls. The Sunwapta River tumbles through a steep-walled limestone gorge, making a sharp turn from northwest to southwest. Follow a 2km (1.2-mile) trail along the north bank of the river for excellent views. *50km (31 miles) north of*

The patio at the Icefields Centre yields great views of the Columbia Icefield.

An aerial view of Sunwapta Falls.

Icefields Centre and 55km (34 miles) south of Jasper Townsite. Follow turnoff to parking lot.

Continue north on the Icefields Parkway, turning northwest or left onto:

5 Hwy. 93A. The Icefields Parkway soon meets Hwy. 93A, a scenic road with less traffic that heads up towards Jasper. It's a good option if you have time. *30km (19 miles) from Jasper and 75km (47 miles) from Icefields Centre.*

Mt. Edith Cavell.

Make a quick left into the parking lot at:

6 ★ Athabasca Falls. The milky-blue Athabasca River pours through a narrow canyon cut out of quartzite rock. A nearby bridge offers phenomenal views of the thundering falls and Mt. Kerkeslin in the background. *Just past the 93A turnoff, on south side of road, 30km (19 miles) south of Jasper and 75km (47 miles) north of the Icefields Centre.*

Continue northwest on 93A. After 8km (5 miles), turn left.

7 ★ Cavell Road. Follow Hwy. 93A north along the west bank of the Athabasca River and over the Whirlpool River to Cavell Road. Turn left. Completed in 1924, this narrow, winding road is challenging to drive and is off-limits to most RVs and trailers (anything over 7m/23 ft.). It is also closed from October through June, depending on snow.

8 Mt. Edith Cavell. At 3,363m (11,033 ft.), Mt. Edith Cavell, named after a World War I heroine, is the highest and arguably most scenic mountain in the vicinity of Jasper Townsite. Angel Glacier saddles the northeastern slope and sends a tongue of ice off the cliff side. *28km (17 miles) from Hwy. 93A on the Cavell Rd.*

9 ★★ The Path of the Glacier Trail. From the parking lot at the base of Mt. Edith Cavell, this trail takes you over boulders, shrubbery, pebbles, and sand through a landscape that, less than a century ago, was covered by a glacier. New plants, trees, shrubs, and wildflowers have slowly returned to the area, known as a terminal moraine. *It's an easy 1.6km (1-mile) loop that will take 45 min.*

Drive back down the Cavell Road and turn left on Hwy. 93A, which will take you back to Jasper.

Maligne Valley Road

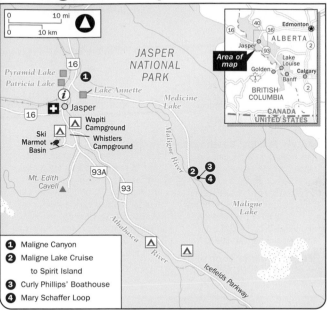

1 Maligne Canyon
2 Maligne Lake Cruise
   to Spirit Island
3 Curly Phillips' Boathouse
4 Mary Schaffer Loop

This road takes you through the **Maligne Valley** and ends at the picturesque Maligne Lake. Wildlife can often be spotted on this half-day outing, including big-horn sheep, deer, elk, moose, grizzly bear, and black bear. With a handful of stops, some short hikes, and a boat cruise, it will take you most of the day. START: **Town of Jasper. Drive east on Connaught Street, turning left onto Hwy. 16. After 4km (2.5 miles), turn south onto Maligne Lake Road.**

1 **Maligne Canyon.** A spectacular example of the cutting power of moving water, this is a very long, gradual waterfall through a deep limestone canyon. There are a series of bridges that take you back and forth down the canyon. *2.3km (1.4 miles) on the Maligne Lake Rd. to Sixth Bridge parking lot.*

Continue on the Maligne Lake Road to its end.

2 ★★ kids **Maligne Lake Cruise to Spirit Island.** This is the best boat tour in the Canadian Rockies. From the deck of the glass-enclosed boats (which are heated on chilly days), watch for eagles, mountain goats, and even the odd avalanche. The cruise makes a stop halfway up the lake at the mysterious Spirit Island and then returns to the dock. *At the end of Maligne Lake Rd.* ☎ 866/625-4463 or 780/852-3370. www.malignelake.com. $55 adults, $27.50 kids 5–14. Cruises depart hourly in summer 10am–5pm.

Looking down at Maligne Canyon.

❸ Curly Phillips' Boathouse. Curly Phillips, a canoe guide and trapper from Ontario, built a floating boathouse on Maligne Lake in 1928 that still stands today. Rent canoes at this historic building for $30 an hour. *Just east of the cafeteria behind the first parking lot on Maligne Lake.* ☎ *780/852-3370.*

❹ Mary Schaffer Loop (also known as Loop Trail). A pleasant hike around the north side of Maligne Lake, the largest lake in the Canadian Rockies, reaches a viewpoint with an interpretive display about explorer Mary Schaffer, the first woman of European descent to set eyes on the lake in 1908 and the most prolific writer about the place. It's a 3.2km (2-mile) loop that will take you just over an hour.

East of Jasper

Miette Hot Springs ★. Head out for one of Jasper's best hikes (the Sulphur Skyline), and then soak your tired bones in these hot mineral pools. From Jasper Townsite, follow the Yellowhead Hwy. 16, 42km (26 miles) east to Miette Road. Follow Miette Road 17km (11 miles) south to the end of the road. ☎ *780/866-3939. Admission $6 adults, $5.15 seniors and children, $18 family pass. Mid-May to 3rd week of June and early Sept to mid-Oct daily 10:30am–9pm; late June to early Sept daily 8:30am–10:30pm. Closed mid-Oct to mid-May.*

Soaking in the Miette Hot Springs.

Town of Jasper

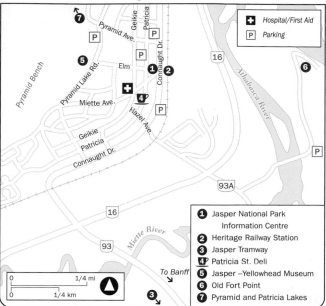

Hospital/First Aid

P Parking

1. Jasper National Park Information Centre
2. Heritage Railway Station
3. Jasper Tramway
4. Patricia St. Deli
5. Jasper –Yellowhead Museum
6. Old Fort Point
7. Pyramid and Patricia Lakes

ocated in the heart of the park, the town of Jasper came into being in anticipation of a transcontinental railway that now runs up the Athabasca Valley and over the Yellowhead Pass. The Canadian National Railway built a series of cabins on the shores of Lac Beauvert, which later became the Jasper Park Lodge. Today, the town feels very different from the Town of Banff—it's less crowded and lacks the swanky shops and nightclubs of its southern counterpart. START: **Jasper Information Centre.**

① **Jasper National Park Information Centre.** In this cozy and central heritage building, get your bearings and get information from the Friends of Jasper, Parks Canada, and Jasper Tourism and Commerce, all of which have booths at the information center. Jasper Tourism and Commerce can tell you about hotel, restaurant, and outfitting options in the park (☎ 780/852-3858). *500 Connaught Dr.* ☎ *780/852-6176.*

Daily Mar 1–June 12, Oct 1–31, and Nov 1–Apr 4 9am–5pm; June 13–Aug 31 8:30am–7pm; Sept 1–30 9am–6pm.

Cross Connaught Street to visit the:

② **Heritage Railway Station.** Like the CIBC Bank building next to the Info Centre, this building is a great example of the rustic Arts and Crafts architecture of its era. Built in

The Jasper National Park Information Centre.

1921 and designated a World Heritage Site in 1991, it now houses park administration as well as the train station. You can still picture Victorian ladies with their parasols and elaborate dresses mixing with rough 'n' tumble gold diggers at this old frontier outpost. In fact, many people still arrive in Jasper here via the ViaRail passenger train. *607 Connaught Dr.*

Drive south 4km (2½ miles) from the townsite, on Hwy. 93A, turn west at Whistlers Road, and

The Jasper–Yellowhead Museum is a great escape on a rainy day.

continue for 2.5km (1½ miles) to the Tramway terminal, following clearly marked signs to:

❸ ★★ kids Jasper Tramway. Your quickest and easiest way to the high alpine terrain, this 7-minute gondola ride takes you up 973m (3,192 ft.), just short of the summit of the Whistlers. From the top, the views of the Athabasca and Miette valleys are stunning. There's a well-marked, though quite steep, 45-minute trail to the summit of the mountain. The view is more outstanding with each step upward. Dress warmly and wear good walking shoes. At the summit, the panoramic view takes in six mountain ranges, including Mt. Robson, the highest point in the Canadian Rockies. Rides leave every 10 minutes or so. ☎ *780/852-3093. www.jasper tramway.com. $31 adults, $16 children 6 to 15, free for children 5 and under. April 7–May 18 daily 10am– 5pm; May 19–June 22 daily 9:30am– 6:30pm; June 23–Aug 26 9am–8pm; Aug 27–Oct 8 10am–5pm. Closed mid-Oct to mid-May.*

Return to town by the same route. Park on Patricia Street.

4 Patricia St. Deli. The best sandwiches—and some of the friendliest people—in Jasper are at this deli right in the heart of town. "Two slices of bread with heaven in between," they say. A hiker's lunch includes chips and cookies for $13 and makes a great picnic. *606 Patricia St.* ☎ *780/852-4814. $.*

Turn left on Pyramid Avenue and left again on Pyramid Lake Road.

5 Jasper–Yellowhead Museum. Good for a rainy day, this museum has exhibits with artifacts from the park's early days, including fur-trade and mountaineering equipment. You'll find legendary guide Curly Phillips's hand-built cedar-strip canoe, Métis beaded deerskin jackets, and the gear used during the first ascent of Mt. Alberta in 1925. *400 Pyramid Lake Rd.* ☎ *780/852-3013. www.jaspermuseum.org. $6 adults; $5 seniors, students, and children 6–18; free for children 5 and under. Daily 10am–5pm in summer. In winter, closed Mon–Wed.*

Drive 5 minutes south of Jasper Townsite via Hwy. 93A or Hazel Avenue, crossing Hwy. 16. Turn east on Old Fort Point Road and park in the first parking lot after the bridge.

6 ★★ Old Fort Point. Climbing the stairs up Old Fort Point is steep, but worthwhile. Jutting out into the Athabasca River, the point offers great views that take in Jasper Townsite, Lac Beauvert, and the Fairmont Jasper Park Lodge. From here you can also catch sight of Kerkeslin and Hardisty mountains to the southeast, and the snowy triangle of Mt. Edith Cavell, shining above all others, to the south. The trail head is just across the river bridge on Old Fort Point Road.

Head back to town, east (right) on Connaught Drive and north (left) on Pyramid Lake Road.

7 Pyramid and Patricia Lakes. Head out in the early evening to spot wildlife on land (elk, deer, and moose) and in the water (beavers and ducks) just above town. Fishing is also a draw. Pyramid Island has a nice, short interpretive loop, great for watching the day come to an end.

The stairs up to Old Fort Point.

Yoho National Park

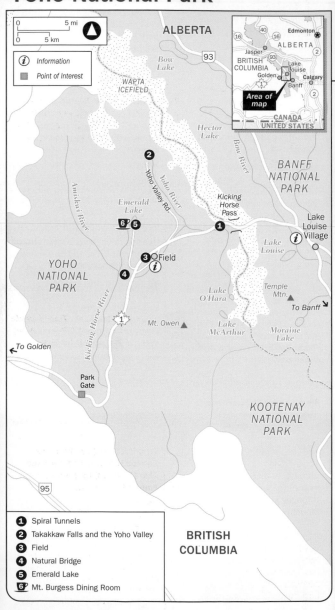

| 0 | 5 mi |
| 0 | 5 km |

(i) Information

■ Point of Interest

ALBERTA

Bow Lake

93

WAPTA ICEFIELD

Hector Lake

Edmonton
16 · 40
16
Jasper
ALBERTA
BRITISH COLUMBIA
93 · 2
Lake Louise
Golden
Calgary
Banff
Area of map
2
CANADA
UNITED STATES

Amiskwi River

Yoho River

Yoho Valley Rd.

Emerald Lake

6 5

3 ○ Field
(i)

4

Kicking Horse River

1

YOHO NATIONAL PARK

Mt. Owen ▲

Kicking Horse Pass

BANFF NATIONAL PARK

Bow River

Lake Louise Village (i)

Lake Louise

Lake O'Hara

Lake McArthur

Temple Mtn. ▲

To Banff ↗

Moraine Lake

← To Golden

Park Gate ■

KOOTENAY NATIONAL PARK

95

1 Spiral Tunnels
2 Takakkaw Falls and the Yoho Valley
3 Field
4 Natural Bridge
5 Emerald Lake
6 Mt. Burgess Dining Room

BRITISH COLUMBIA

Yoho National Park makes a great base for exploring the Rockies. You're midway between the Columbia Icefield and the Town of Banff, next door to Lake Louise, and yet in a less-traveled area. "Yoho" is an expression of awe and wonder in the Cree language, and that's just what you'll experience in the park. This drive takes you from Lake Louise southwest on the Trans-Canada Hwy. 1 through the park toward Golden, BC. START: **Lake Louise.**

A freight train passes through the spiral tunnels of Kicking Horse Pass.

Take the Trans-Canada Hwy. 1 west from Lake Louise 9.2km (5¾ miles) to the border between Alberta and British Columbia. Continue 8.7km (5½ miles) west of the border and turn off into the roadside interpretive display at the:

❶ ★ Spiral Tunnels. The first trains to make it over Kicking Horse Pass had really difficult ascents going toward Lake Louise, or wild rides descending the steep west slope. Engineers developed a groundbreaking plan to ease the incline: The Spiral Tunnels take trains through two loops inside Cathedral Mountain, easing the steepness substantially. View the Spiral Tunnels from two lookouts: The first (and best) is on the side of Trans-Canada Hwy. 1 just up the hill from Field and has excellent interpretive signs; the second is on Yoho Valley Road just past the Cathedral Mountain Lodge.

Continue down the hill on the Trans-Canada Highway another 3.7km (2⅓ miles), turning right at Yoho Valley Road. Continue on to the end.

❷ ★★ Takakkaw Falls and the Yoho Valley. If you love waterfalls, you've come to the right place: "Takakkaw" means magnificent in Cree. At 380m (1,247 ft.), this is the fourth-highest waterfall in Canada and originates at the Daly Glacier high above. There's a great picnic spot at the base. Looking to the north, you can often see the Yoho Glacier on a clear day. This is also the trail head for some superb hiking.

Drive back out to the Trans-Canada Hwy. 1, continuing 1.8km (1 mile) west to the turnoff for Field.

❸ ★ Field. This tiny town is the service center for Yoho National Park. It makes a good place to stop for lunch but isn't worth a visit in and of itself. Grab a sandwich, a coffee, and maybe pop into the pottery shop, and keep moving.

Turn left (west) on the Trans-Canada Highway and continue 2km (1¼ miles) to the turnoff for Emerald Lake Road.

❹ Natural Bridge. Just south of Field is the Natural Bridge, where the Kicking Horse River meets with U-shape sedimentary rock that has so far kept the river from breaking open a deep canyon. The river did manage to erode a small canyon of softer rock just upstream from the tougher section, creating a crooked

Lake O'Hara: Getting to Paradise

In Yoho National Park, the best hiking trails are at magical Lake O'Hara, a region that makes some locals misty-eyed just at its mention. There are some easy, shorter hikes around the lake itself, and a handful of excellent 3- to 6-hour trails that take you above Lake O'Hara to some of the equally spectacular surrounding lakes. The best bet is to connect all the short hikes into a challenging day hike known as the ★★★ **Lake O'Hara Alpine Circuit** (p 4).

Just on the other side of Lake Louise, O'Hara is accessed by a 13km (8-mile) road that can be hiked or cross-country skied in the winter. But daily Parks Canada–run bus rides (from mid-June to mid-Oct) will take you up to the warden station on the shores of Lake O'Hara in a painless 15 minutes. That'll give you the rest of the day for hiking. You must reserve a spot on the bus by calling ☎ **250/343-6433.** Do this well ahead of time (reservations are accepted beginning Apr 1) because the bus fills up completely—space is very limited. There are no restrictions on the number of people hiking the somewhat boring access road.

While you're on the line, you can also reserve a campsite at the Lake O'Hara Campground if you plan on staying the night at the lake. It's a good spot for families—it's in the backcountry, but accessible by bus so you don't have to worry about carrying everything in on your back.

Bus tickets cost $15 for adults and $7.30 for children, round-trip. Buses leave the parking lot daily at 8:30 and 10:30am. The last bus out departs the campground at 6:30pm.

The parking lot is located 1km (½ mile) west of the Alberta–British Columbia border, just off the south side of the Trans-Canada Hwy. 1. Turn south at the sign to Lake O'Hara and west into the parking lot. You must reserve campsites well in advance; the reservation line opens April 1. For more information, visit www.pc.gc.ca/yoho. Lake O'Hara Lodge has its own private bus service for its guests (p 137).

Hiking on the Lake O'Hara Alpine Circuit.

The Kicking Horse River passes underneath the Natural Bridge.

bridge. Visit it soon—it may be gone in a matter of centuries!

Drive 7km (4⅓ miles) until you reach:

❺ ★★ Emerald Lake. Farther up the road from the Natural Bridge is the spectacular glacier-fed Emerald Lake, featuring hiking trails, canoe rentals, horse stables, and the lovely Emerald Lake Lodge (see "Where to Stay in Yoho National Park," p 137). A visit to Emerald Lake will fill you with wonder, and could fill an album worth of photos.

❻ Mt. Burgess Dining Room. Finish the day on a high note. The seasonal fine dining inside this historic lodge is all about rustic Rocky Mountain cuisine with artistic flare. The menu focuses on local game like elk, bison, and caribou, and there's an award-winning wine list with over 400 labels. *It's part of Emerald Lake Lodge. On Emerald Lake Rd., 8km (5 miles) off Trans-Canada Hwy. 1, at a turnoff 2km (1¼ miles) south of Field.* ☎ 250/343-6321. $$$.

The Burgess Shale

The Rockies' greatest contribution to archaeology is the 515-million-year-old Burgess Shale, a fossil bed discovered at the base of Mt. Stephen. This discovery transformed our understanding of the evolution of life on Earth and gave real examples of the amazing biodiversity that existed before the mass extinction of species—half of the animal groups seen in the shale have since disappeared from Earth. You can get there to see them only on a 6-hour, 6km (3¾-mile) guided hike organized by the Yoho Burgess Shale Foundation. This is a must for archaeology buffs, but you cannot drive to the Burgess Shale or visit it on your own; you must hike in to the site on an official tour with a registered guide. You will not enjoy this trip unless you are quite fit. Kids will enjoy the shorter hike to the Mt. Stephen Fossil Beds.

Reserve in advance at www.burgess-shale.bc.ca or ☎ 800/343-3006 or 250/343-3006. Hike costs $120 adults, $65 students, $25 children 11 and under. It's available Friday through Monday from July 1 through Sept 15. The group takes only 15 fit hikers on one trip per day.

Golden, British Columbia

1 Eagle's Eye Gondola and Grizzly Bear Refuge

2 Mountain Biking at Kicking Horse Mountain Resort

3 Rafting the Kicking Horse River

4 Bacchus Books

5 Moberly Marshes

Golden is located just off the Trans-Canada Highway (Hwy. 1) at the confluence of the Kicking Horse and Columbia rivers. The small town (pop. 4,200) has been on the verge of a boom for several years as it shifts gears from a resource-based economy to one based on outdoor recreation. This is largely due to the recently redeveloped Kicking Horse Mountain Resort (frequently ranked as one of the best ski resorts in North America). Although it is not located within Yoho National Park (it's 20km/12 miles west of the park), Golden is the park's major gateway and service center. **START: Kicking Horse Mountain Resort is 14km (8⅔ miles) from Golden on Kicking Horse Trail Road.**

1 ★★ **Eagle's Eye Gondola and Grizzly Bear Refuge.** Soar up to 2,350m (7,710 ft.) for a panoramic view of the Rocky and Purcell mountains. Hike the Terminator Ridge. Friday evenings and some Saturdays, the gorgeous restaurant opens for high altitude a la carte dining. Combine a gondola ride with a visit to the world's largest enclosed and protected grizzly bear refuge near the gondola's base. It's where Boo the grizzly lives and plays. *From Hwy. 95, turn west at blue sign for Kicking Horse Mountain Resort in downtown Golden, 13km/8 miles uphill.* ☎ *866/ 754-5425 or 250/439-5424. www. kickinghorseresort.com. Gondola only: $27 adults, $24 ages 13–18 and seniors, $16 kids 12 and under. Grizzly Bear Refuge: $21.50 adults, $19 seniors, $15.50 youth 13–17,*

A resident at the Grizzly Bear refuge.

$11 kids 6–13, free kids 5 and under. June 29–Sept 2 Sun–Thurs 11am–4:30pm, Fri–Sat 10:30am–4:30pm.

❷ Mountain Biking. When the snow leaves Kicking Horse Mountain Resort, the trails and the lifts are opened to two-wheelers for world-class downhill biking. Stick your bike on the gondola and cruise down twisty single-track trails. *At the base of Kicking Horse Mountain Resort.* ☎ *866/754-5425 or 250/439-5424. www.kickinghorseresort.com. Full-day bike ticket costs $43 adults, $37 youth and seniors, $21 kids 7–12.*

From Kicking Horse Mountain Resort, head back into Golden. Drive through town and up the hill on Trans-Canada Hwy. 1. Twenty-five kilometers (16 miles) from Golden, turn right at the sign for Beaverfoot Lodge.

❸ White-Water Rafting. The rapids on the Kicking Horse River are some of the best in British Columbia. You'll dive through narrow canyons

and see the valley from a totally different perspective. Plus, it's buckets of fun! Kootenay River Runners runs a half-day trip along the river. *1km/⅔ mile west of the western gates of Kootenay National Park.* ☎ *800/599-4399 or 250/347-9210. www.kootenayriverrunners.com. Rates are $90 with lunch. Children age 13 and under not permitted.*

Back in Golden, turn right onto 6th Avenue and take a quick left onto 9th Street.

❹ Bacchus Books. Sure, the eclectic first floor is chock-a-block with unique (and distracting!) books, but follow your nose upstairs to the cafe and you'll discover fresh baked treats, natural and thick homemade soups, a roasted veggie panini, or a smoked turkey wrap. *409 9th Ave. N.* ☎ *250/344-5600. www.bacchusbooks.ca. $.*

❺ Kids Moberly Marshes. The Gadsden Provincial Park houses a wetland that stretches for 180km (112 miles) and is the largest remaining wetlands area in North America. Since this is home to more than 260 resident and migratory bird species, you may also spot deer, elk, beavers, muskrats, and mink. Bring your binoculars and stroll along the dikes. *10km (6.2 miles) north of Golden along Trans Canada Hwy. 1.*

White-water rafting on the Kicking Horse River.

Kootenay National Park

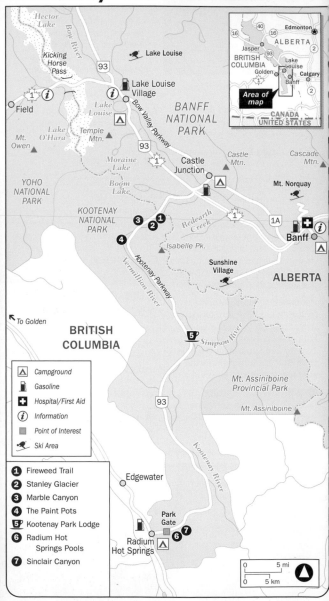

Area of map

Legend:

- ⌂ Campground
- ⛽ Gasoline
- ✚ Hospital/First Aid
- ⓘ Information
- ▪ Point of Interest
- 🎿 Ski Area

1. Fireweed Trail
2. Stanley Glacier
3. Marble Canyon
4. The Paint Pots
5. Kootenay Park Lodge
6. Radium Hot Springs Pools
7. Sinclair Canyon

0 — 5 mi
0 — 5 km

A drive through **Kootenay National Park makes a great day trip from Banff National Park.** Established in 1920, the park is quite long and narrow (94km/58 miles long; 8km/5 miles across) and has a remarkably diverse landscape. The main road through the park traverses the scars of the massive 2003 forest fire; two large lightning-caused fires eventually merged and burned 12.6% of the park. It's a quiet park, with some interesting stops along the 94km (58-mile) Banff–Windermere Highway. It'll take you about 90 minutes to drive back from Radium Hot Springs directly to Banff, but this tour runs southwest, starting at the border of Banff National Park. **START: Castle Junction, Banff National Park.**

Trees along the Fireweed Trail.

Take Hwy. 93 west towards British Columbia.

1 **kids** **Fireweed Trail.** Just past the Continental Divide and over the Alberta–British Columbia border, make a stop at the Vermillion Pass to hike the Fireweed Trail, a short 20-minute loop with interpretive signs that explain why natural forest fires are healthy and good for the environment and are no longer suppressed by Parks Canada. *On the south side of Hwy. 93, at the provincial border.*

Continue west on Hwy. 93.

2 **★★ Stanley Glacier.** Taking you from fire to ice in only 2.5km (1½ miles), this is a relatively short and only moderately steep half-day hike on the crest of the Continental Divide. The family-friendly trail takes you up to a hanging valley with a giant glacier clinging to the limestone cliffs at the back. There are great views throughout the entire hike. Great in the morning. *On the south side of Hwy. 93, 3.2km (2 miles) past the provincial border.*

Continue west on Hwy. 93.

3 **★★ Marble Canyon.** If it's a hot day, you'll particularly enjoy a short hike at this narrow trail of limestone carved by two retreated glaciers. The farther up the trail you walk,

Water flowing through Marble Canyon.

Vintage cars parked outside the Kootenay Park Lodge.

Radium

A small town (population 675) at the southern end of Kootenay National Park, Radium Hot Springs—often simply called Radium—is named for (you guessed it) its famous hot springs, which draw visitors to soak in their supposedly healing waters. The town is essentially a strip of motels and restaurants, but if you explore some of the back roads you'll discover a spectacular setting and bump into more than a few Calgary residents who make this their second home. It's also a good area for golfing and hiking—the **Radium Resort** (☎ 800/667-6444 or 250/347-6200; www.radiumresort. com) has an 18-hole championship course located along the cliffs that border the Columbia River, or you can hike the Juniper Trail past Sinclair Canyon or the Valley View Trail which starts at Redstreak Campground.

The popular Radium Hot Springs have been in business since 1914.

the more impressive the canyon. It's cool and shady here. And don't be fooled by the name: There is no marble, only white and gray dolomite rock. Kids will find the hike intriguing, but keep an eye on them because the trail can get very slippery. *On the north side of Hwy. 93, 7km (4⅓ miles) past the provincial border.*

Continue west on Hwy. 93.

❹ **The Paint Pots.** A brief and beautiful walk takes you to this fascinating area where First Nations people gathered ocher, an iron-based mineral that was baked, crushed, mixed with grease, and used as a paint for tepees, pictographs, and personal adornment. There is an excellent, wheelchair-friendly, 30-minute interpretive trail. *On the north side of Hwy. 93, 10km (6¼ miles) past the provincial border.*

5 **Kootenay Park Lodge.** The only place to stop and grab a bite to eat inside Kootenay National Park is at this historic lodge. Try the homemade burgers and "mountain fries." There's a Parks Canada–run information center next door with snacks, maps, and a friendly staff.

Hwy. 93 at Vermillion Crossing, 42km (26 miles) west of Castle Junction, 61km (38 miles) east of Radium Hot Springs. ☎ *403/762-9196. $$.*

Continue west on Hwy. 93.

❻ ★ **Radium Hot Springs Pools.** These "sacred mountain waters" have been drawing visitors to the Columbia Valley since 1914. There is one hot pool (104°F/40°C); and a cooler pool (81°F/27°C), both settled in a canyon rich with oxide, giving the walls a permanent orange-sunset look. *3km (1¾ miles) northeast of the Town of Radium on Hwy. 93.* ☎ *800/767/1611 or 250/347-9485. Admission $6.50 adults, $5.50 seniors and children. Mid-May to mid-Oct daily 9am– 11pm; mid-Oct to mid-May Sun– Thurs noon–9pm, Fri–Sat noon–10pm.*

Continue west on Hwy. 93.

❼ **Sinclair Canyon.** Kootenay closes with a bang at the spectacular red cliffs of Sinclair Canyon, which welcome you to the Columbia Valley just after the Radium Hot Springs pools.

Cars pass through the red cliffs of Sinclair Canyon.

Calgary in One Day

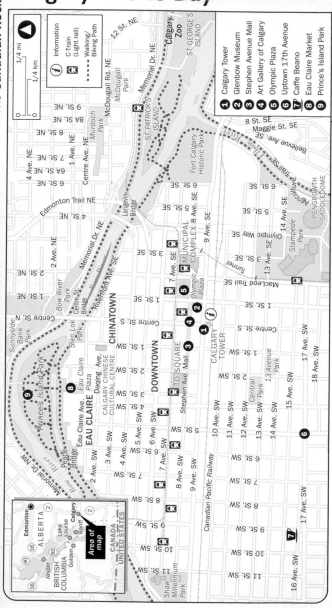

Information

ⓘ Information

CK C-Train (Light rail)

••••• Walking/Biking Path

1 Calgary Tower
2 Glenbow Museum
3 Stephen Avenue Mall
4 Art Gallery of Calgary
5 Olympic Plaza
6 Uptown 17th Avenue
7 Caffe Beano
8 Eau Claire Market
9 Prince's Island Park

With over a million people, a strong economy, and plenty of personality, Calgary is stepping boldly into its role as the "heart of the New West." Safe, clean, and young, Calgary has an identity that goes beyond white cowboy hats and rodeos. And while hipsters may snicker at the cowboy schtick, it is really authentic here. Western hospitality is legendarily friendly, upbeat, and relaxed. It's a fun and exciting city that is quite simple to discover. With a day or two, you can take in the main sites and have a bit of time to wander in one of the city's top neighborhoods—Kensington or Inglewood stand out. START: **Calgary Tower.**

The Calgary Tower and the Calgary skyline.

❶ ★★ **Calgary Tower.** Come here first to get your bearings 191m (627 ft.) in the sky. You can spot the Stampede Grounds and Pengrowth Saddledome (where the NHL's Calgary Flames play) to the southwest, the Bow River winding through town, and the snow-capped Rocky Mountains on the western horizon. *9th Ave. and Centre St.* ☎ *403/266-7171. www.calgarytower.com. Elevator ride $16 adults, $14 seniors, $11 youth 13–17, $7 children 4–12. June–Aug daily 9am–10pm; Sept–May daily 9am–9pm.*

Walk 1 block east on 9th Ave. SE, turning left on 1st SE.

❷ **Glenbow Museum.** The walls and halls of this storied museum downtown tell the story of the West,

from the past to the present. Start in the Blackfoot Gallery to learn about First Nations cultures; then

A public art installation in the Stephen Avenue Mall.

Olympic Plaza.

continue on to the Mavericks Gallery, which celebrates today's groundbreakers. *130 9th Ave. SE, at 1st St. ☎ 403/268-4100. www. glenbow.org. Admission $14 adults, $10 seniors, $9 students and youth. Mon–Sat 9am–5pm; Sun noon–5pm.*

Turn left on 1st Street SE and left again at 8th Avenue SE, also known as Stephen Avenue.

❸ **Stephen Avenue Mall.** A pedestrian avenue that is lined by banks, high-end shops like Holt Renfrew and Birks, lively eateries, and some interesting public art, this is a great spot for lunch. Try **Charcut** (899 Centre S. S.; ☎ 403/984-2180) for butcher steaks, the fashionable **Belvedere** (107 8th Ave. SW; ☎ 403/265-9595), or the chic **Blink** (111 8th Ave. SW; ☎ 403/263-5330).

The patio at Prince's Island's River Café.

❹ **Art Gallery of Calgary.** Contemporary art's home in Calgary is in a historic building on convenient Stephen Avenue Mall. Evolving exhibits showcase a variety of mediums. *117 8th Ave. SW. ☎ 403/770-1350. www.artgallerycalgary.org. Admission by donation. Tues–Sat 10am–5pm.*

Walk past 1st Street SE to the far east end of Stephen Avenue.

❺ **Olympic Plaza.** A public square across the street from Calgary's stately, sandstone Old City Hall is at the eastern end of Stephen Avenue. Built for the medal ceremonies of the 1988 Winter Olympics, this is where Calgarians come to celebrate everything from hockey victories to Reggaefest. In winter, there's an outdoor skating rink. *228 8th Ave. SE. ☎ 403/268-2489. Free admission.*

From Stephen Avenue, turn left on 1st SW and walk 7 blocks south.

❻ **Uptown 17th Avenue.** Cross south and venture through a gentrifying neighborhood towards the eclectic, funky stretch of 17th Avenue. Fashion boutiques, vintage stores, clubs, coffee shops, and great bistros draw fashionistas, foodies, and those just looking for a nice stroll. *17th Ave. SW btw. 10th St. and 4th St. SW.*

❼ **Caffe Beano.** At the corner of 17th Avenue and 9th Street, stop in here for a steaming latte. Espresso milkshakes will also pick you up. *1613 9th St. SW.* ☎ *403/229-1232. $.*

Hop in a cab or turn left at 4th Street SW and walk north 13 blocks, turning right on 2nd Avenue SW.

8 Eau Clair Market. It's lacking some of its former freshness, but there is still lots of action happening around this complex on the edge of Calgary's downtown business core. Family-friendly pizza places, pubs, and nightclubs line the outside; specialty shops are inside. The food court is a good place for a cheap meal, and there's a movie theater upstairs. *200 Barclay Parade SW. www.eauclairemarket.com. Market building 9am–9pm; shops and restaurants have varied hours.*

From behind the Market, pass the fountain and head on to the bridge over the Bow River.

9 Prince's Island Park. Where Calgarians come to stretch, run, bike, rollerblade, stroll, and play, this urban island can be beautiful on a warm spring or summer evening. A network of paths follows the Bow River and connects with various arteries of the city. At the heart of the island is the outstanding River Café (p 124). *Near 2nd Ave. SW and 3rd St. SW.*

Calgary Stampede

If you're in Calgary during the first 2 weeks of July, well, yee-haw! The world-famous Calgary Stampede, calling itself the "Greatest Outdoor Show on Earth," takes over the city in a major way. It's the richest rodeo around, with $2 million in prizes. From morning stampede breakfasts and parades to a roller-coaster midway and live concerts, there is a lot to soak in. Visit www.calgarystampede.com for more information on the event and how to get tickets.

The rodeo at the Calgary Stampede is the most lucrative on the circuit.

Calgary in Two Days

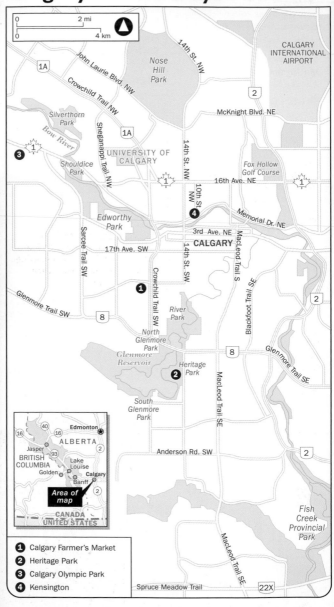

1 Calgary Farmer's Market

2 Heritage Park

3 Calgary Olympic Park

4 Kensington

You've seen all the main highlights of Calgary and its bustling downtown core. A second day will let you branch out to roam the wider regions of Calgary. But you'll need a vehicle for today's trip. START: **Calgary Farmer's Market, where you can grab a healthy breakfast.**

❶ Calgary Farmer's Market. A year-round indoor market has rows and rows of seasonal produce, organic meat, and artwork from more than 100 vendors. *510–77 Ave SE.* ☎ *403/240-9113. Free admission. Thurs–Sun 9am–5pm.*

Continue south on Crowchild Trail, turning east on Glenmore Trail. Turn south on 14th Street SW into the Glenmore Park.

❷ Heritage Park. A re-created pioneer village covers the years from 1860 to 1940. Ride on a steam train or paddlewheeler, or go for a ride on the antique midway. *1900 Heritage Dr. SW.* ☎ *403/268-8500. Adults $25, children 3–17 $19, families $87. May 19–Sept 3 daily 9am–5pm; rest of year Sat–Sun 9am–5pm.*

Head north out of Glenmore Park onto 14th Street SW, turning west or left on Glenmore Trail. Follow until it meets up with the Trans-Canada Hwy. 1. Go west to the next exit.

❸ Calgary Olympic Park. The slopes that hosted luge, bobsleigh, and ski jumping in the 1988 Olympics has a small ski hill open to all during the winter. In summer, it turns into a playground with mountain biking, zip-lining, and great views from the top of the Ski Jump Tower. There's also an Olympic museum and Canada's Sports Hall of Fame. *88 Canada Olympic Rd. SW.* ☎ *403/247-5452. Free admission; pay per activity. Hours vary.*

Take the Trans-Canada Hwy. 1 east back towards the city. Turn east at Memorial Drive, following the Bow River until you reach Kensington Road.

❹ Kensington. To mix and mingle with Calgarians, head to Kensington Road. There are pubs, cafes, unique boutiques, some excellent restaurants—**Globefish,** on 14th Street just north of Kensington Road (☎ 403/521-0221) has the best sushi in Calgary—and a relaxed feel in one of the city's liveliest neighborhoods.

Calgary Olympic Park offers lots of activities and Canada's Sports Hall of Fame.

Calgary **Dining & Lodging**

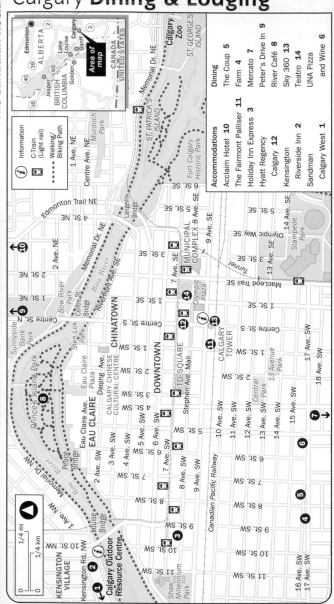

Dining
The Coup **5**
Farm **4**
Mercato **7**
Peter's Drive In **9**
River Café **8**
Sky 360 **13**
Teatro **14**
UNA Pizza
and Wine **6**

Accommodations
Acclaim Hotel **10**
The Fairmont Palliser **11**
Holiday Inn Express **3**
Hyatt Regency
Calgary **12**
Kensington
Riverside Inn **2**
Sandman
Calgary West **1**

Information

C-Train
(Light rail)

Walking/
Biking Path

Dining & Lodging A to Z

Restaurants

★ **The Coup** 17th AVENUE *VEGE-TARIAN* Healthy, fresh, creative fusion food stars at this hip spot on 17th Avenue. Most ingredients are vegetarian, organic, and local. There are jampacked salads, falafel quesadillas, and a dragon bowl that has steamed veggies, tofu, and brown rice. There's also a fun cocktail list. *924 17th Ave. SW. ☎ 403/541-1041. www.thecoup.ca. Entrees $13–$16. AE, MC, V. Tues–Thurs 11:30am–3pm and 5–10pm; Fri 11:30am–3pm and 5–11pm; Sat 9am–3pm and 5–11pm; Sun 9am–3pm and 5–9pm. Map p 122.*

★ **Farm** 17th AVENUE *REGIONAL* Just as the name suggests, this a place to sample wholesome, simple food. It's classic "slow food" style, but it's more precious than most pastoral country tables. Small plates and platters make sampling from the outstanding cheese selection a good idea. The mac 'n' cheese is the best in town. The ambience is as relaxing as the countryside. *1006 17th Ave. SW. ☎ 403/245-2276. www.farm-restaurant.com. Entrees $14–$24. AE, MC, V. Daily 11:30am–10pm. Map p 122.*

★ **Mercato** MISSION *ITALIAN* Inside Calgary's swanky gourmet Italian deli, the restaurant is mainly counter-style. The simplified Italian food, however, is show-stealing, particularly the *bisteca fiorentina* rib-eye steak. It's an energetic, sometimes frantic place a few blocks from 17th Avenue in the upscale 4th Street–Mission district. *2224 4th St. SW. ☎ 403/263-5535. www.mercatogourmet.com. Entrees $16–$44. AE, MC, V. Daily 11:30am–2pm and 5:30–9pm. Map p 122.*

kids **Peter's Drive In** NORTH OF DOWNTOWN *DINER* If you're en route to Banff from the Calgary airport (or vice versa), drop by this legendary and truly retro (it's been around since 1964) "drive-in" just off the Trans-Canada Highway for burgers, fries, onion rings, and a shake. You can be served in the car or go through the drive-through window. *219 16th Ave. ☎ 403/277-2747. www.petersdrivein.com. Entrees $4–$5. No credit cards. Daily 9am–midnight. Map p 122.*

★★ **River Café** PRINCE'S ISLAND PARK *REGIONAL* From the picturesque setting in a wooden lodge on an island in the Bow River to a menu that exemplifies regional and seasonal Alberta cuisine, this is a rich experience. Start with the emblematic fish and game platter. Then opt for bison or beef. If you're only in town for 1 night and it's not storming

The open-concept kitchen at Farm.

out, then this should be your choice for dinner. *Prince's Island Park.* ☎ *403/261-7670. www.river-cafe. com. Entrees $26–$49. AE, MC, V. Mon–Fri 11am–11pm; Sat–Sun 10am–11pm. Map p 122.*

★ **Sky 360** DOWNTOWN *REGIONAL* There's more than just spectacular views 762 steps up from the ground in the Calgary Tower. The menu is now much more gourmet-focused and upscale, but is also full of crowd-pleasers like goat-cheese penne, grilled salmon, tenderloins, and strip-loins. The elevator fee is included, the wine list excellent, and with the place rotating on a 45-minute schedule, you'll get a couple of full city views and time to relax. *In the Calgary Tower. 101 9th Ave. SW. ☎ 403/532-7966. www.sky360.ca. Entrees $23–$43. AE, MC, V. Mon–Sun 11am–2pm and 5–9pm. Map p 122.*

★★ **Teatro** DOWNTOWN *EURO-PEAN* For a refined, romantic meal, come to this dazzling room inside the historic Dominion Bank building. It's mainly Italian food, since the owner is Italian, but there's a delicate high-end French influence. Pastas come with duck Bolognese or Atlantic lobster sauces, for example. Drop in for a martini or a glass of wine before going to a show, or for

Teatro is located inside the historic Dominion Bank building.

a nightcap. *200 8th Ave. SE, Olympic Plaza. ☎ 403/290-1012. www. teatro.ca. Entrees $24–$49. AE, DC, MC, V. Mon–Fri 11:30am–10pm; Sat–Sun 5–10pm. Map p 122.*

★★ **UNA Pizza and Wine** 17TH AVENUE *PIZZA* Great service, fabulously simple Italian food, a casual and bustling atmosphere, NHL hockey players possibly sitting nearby, even a kids' menu—the only problem at UNA is that you can't make reservations. Come before 6pm or after 7:30pm, or be prepared to stroll 17th Ave while you wait. *618 17th Avenue SW. ☎ 403/453-1183. www.una pizzeria.com. Entrees $15–$19. MC, V. Daily 11:30am–1am. Map p 122.*

Accommodations
Acclaim Hotel AIRPORT If all you need is a good bed before or after your flight, this stylish airport hotel is a great choice. Complimentary shuttle, big fluffy beds, a rooftop hot tub, and a fitness club will ease your travel-weary bones. It's way out of town, though. *123 Freeport Blvd. NE. ☎ 866/955-0008 or 403/291-8000. www.acclaimhotel.ca. 123 units. Doubles $150–$325. AE, MC, V. Map p 122.*

★ **The Fairmont Palliser** DOWNTOWN Opened in 1914, this historic landmark has deep roots in the Calgary community. Rooms here are notoriously cramped, as in most urban hotels of this vintage, but they retain an old-world elegance typical of Fairmont. The new Fairmont Gold rooms have extra value with a private concierge, private check-in, and separate dining area. The lobby could use some freshening up. *133 9th Ave. SW. ☎ 800/441-1414 or 403/262-1234. www.fairmont.com. 407 units. Doubles $149–$549. AE, DC, DISC, MC, V. Map p 122.*

kids Holiday Inn Express DOWNTOWN My choice for best midrange hotel in town, this

The dining area at the Hyatt Regency Calgary.

includes the predictable high-rise hotel experience found in many hotels, plus breakfast. The rooms are average and the location good. There's a small fitness center. Kids eat free in the grill next door. *1020 8th Ave.* ☎ *877/660-8550 or 403/269-8262. www.hiexpress.com. 56 units. Doubles $198–$252. AE, MC, DC, V. Map p 122.*

Hyatt Regency Calgary DOWNTOWN   Of all the chains downtown, this is probably the best. That's because it's the newest and because it's stylishly tucked right into the facade of the historic Stephen Avenue Mall. Rooms are very large. The amazing Stillwater Spa is worth checking out. *700 Centre St.* ☎ *800/233-1234 or 403/717-1234. www.calgary.hyatt.com. 355 units. Doubles $399–$439. AE, MC, DC, V. Map p 122.*

★★ Kensington Riverside Inn KENSINGTON   With more flair and personality than just about every other hotel in town, this boutique inn—on the north side of the river a short walk from downtown—is private, expensive, design-forward, and chic. The rooms are large, the ambience cool, and the new restaurant possibly the hottest in town. *1126 Memorial Dr. NW.* ☎ *877/313-3733 or 403/228-4442. www.kensingtonriversideinn.com. 19 units. Doubles $299–$399. AE, DC, MC, V. Map p 122.*

Sandman Calgary West WEST OF DOWNTOWN   Across the road from Canada Olympic Park, this is the last hotel in town before you hit the road to Banff. It's entirely functional, with an indoor pool and a 24-hour restaurant. If you want a place to crash before hitting the road or if you want to beat traffic in or out of town, this is a good bet. It's 20 minutes from downtown. *125 Bowridge Dr.* ☎ *800/726-3626 or 403/288-6033. www.sandmanhotels.com. 121 units. Doubles $199–$239. AE, MC, V. Map p 122.*

The stylish Kensington Riverside Inn.

126

The Canadian Rockies

Alberta Rockies **Dining & Lodging**

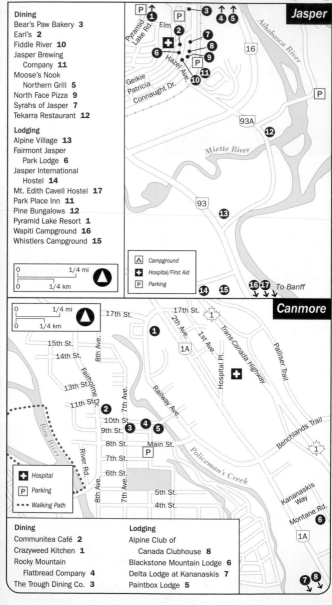

Jasper

Dining
Bear's Paw Bakery **3**
Earl's **2**
Fiddle River **10**
Jasper Brewing
  Company **11**
Moose's Nook
  Northern Grill **5**
North Face Pizza **9**
Syrahs of Jasper **7**
Tekarra Restaurant **12**

Lodging
Alpine Village **13**
Fairmont Jasper
  Park Lodge **6**
Jasper International
  Hostel **14**
Mt. Edith Cavell Hostel **17**
Park Place Inn **11**
Pine Bungalows **12**
Pyramid Lake Resort **1**
Wapiti Campground **16**
Whistlers Campground **15**

Pyramid Lake Rd. Elm
Hazel Ave.
Geikie
Patricia
Connaught Dr.

Athabasca River
16
93A
Miette River
93

0   1/4 mi
0   1/4 km

△ Campground
✚ Hospital/First Aid
P Parking

To Banff

Canmore

17th St.
17th St.
15th St.
14th St.
13th St.
11th St.
Fairholme Dr.
Bow River
River Rd.
10th St.
9th St.
8th St.
7th St.
6th St.
5th St.
4th St.
8th Ave.
7th Ave.
8th Ave.
Main St.
Railway Ave.
2th Ave.
1st Ave.
Trans-Canada Highway
Hospital Pl.
Policeman's Creek
Palliser Trail
Benchlands Trail
Kananaskis Way
Montane Rd.
1
1A
1A

0   1/4 mi
0   1/4 km

✚ Hospital
P Parking
• • • Walking Path

Dining
Communitea Café **2**
Crazyweed Kitchen **1**
Rocky Mountain
  Flatbread Company **4**
The Trough Dining Co. **3**

Lodging
Alpine Club of
  Canada Clubhouse **8**
Blackstone Mountain Lodge **6**
Delta Lodge at Kananaskis **7**
Paintbox Lodge **5**

Dining & Lodging A to Z

Bear's Paw Bakery.

Restaurants

Bear's Paw Bakery JASPER *BAKERY/CAFE* With two locations, this bakery is very popular. There are fresh sandwiches, granola to go, superb fruit tarts, and a huge variety of cookies, bars, and yummy delights—including dog treats. Their freshly baked bread is served at nearly every restaurant in town. *610 Connaught Dr. and 4 Cedar Ave.*

☎ *780/852-3233. www.bearspaw bakery.com. Sandwiches $7–$12. AE, MC, V. Daily 7am–6pm. Map p 126.*

★★ Communitea Café CANMORE *CAFE/VEGETARIAN* Choose from more than 80 blends of loose-leaf tea at this funky hangout. Lunches are healthy, affordable, and tasty. Build your own rice bowl with organic brown rice, steamed veggies, and flavorful Asian sauces. There are also great snacks like sushi, shrimp rolls, organic edamame—and quite possibly the best lattes in town, brewed in a one-of-a-kind espresso machine. This is a place with heart. *117–1001 6th Ave., corner of 10th St.* ☎ *403/678-6818. www.thecommunitea.com. Entrees $8–$14. MC, V. Mon–Fri 9am–4pm; Sat–Sun 9am–5pm. Map p 126.*

★ Crazyweed Kitchen CANMORE *GLOBAL/FUSION* Slightly unpredictable and always provocative, the Crazyweed's new location is both chaotic and creative. The food here could just be the most incredible of your life, particularly the kashmiri lamb balls and the Thai grilled chicken. But service is erratic, either pompously absent or delightfully charming. *1600 Railway Ave.*

The chaotic Crazyweed Kitchen.

☎ 403/609-2530. www.crazyweed.ca. *Entrees $21–$38. AE, MC, V. Daily 11:30am–3pm; Daily 5–10pm. Map p 126.*

Earl's JASPER *CANADIAN* A real crowd-pleaser, Earl's is a good choice for just about anybody—families, couples, or friends. Part of a popular Western Canada chain, there's a bit of Mexican, Asian, and European served here, from burgers to Thai curries to brick-oven pizzas. They also have the nicest outdoor patio in town, including heaters on a chilly evening. *600 Patricia St., upstairs. ☎ 780/852-2393. www. earls.ca. Reservations recommended in summer. Entrees $16–$32. AE, MC, V. Daily 11:30am–midnight. Map p 126.*

Fiddle River JASPER *CANADIAN* Upstairs, above Connaught Street, there's an ever-changing menu here that almost always has Canadiana favorites like Alberta-raised beef, caribou meatloaf, and a steaming bison stew, as well as pumpkin-seed trout and a seafood kettle. The service is casual and friendly, and the views are divine. *620 Connaught St., upstairs. ☎ 780/852-3032. www. fiddleriverrestaurant.com. Entrees $22–$39. AE, MC, V. Daily 5pm–midnight. Map p 126.*

Jasper Brewing Company JASPER *BREWPUB* A warm and cozy place for a pint and a burger, the bartender will suggest the fish and chips or sirloin steak burger. There are big-screen TVs and a cozy fireplace. Highly regarded ales, pilsners, and stouts are brewed in the back; a sample of six costs $15. *624 Connaught Dr. ☎ 780/852-4111. www.jasperbrewingco.com. Entrees $11–$26. AE, MC, V. Daily 11:30am–1am. Map p 126.*

★★ Moose's Nook Northern Grill JASPER *REGIONAL* The best meal in Jasper is to be had at the Jasper Park Lodge's second-tier restaurant (after the white-glove Edith Cavell Dining Room), open summers only. With unforgettable meals like boar bacon–wrapped bison tenderloin, great service, and live jazz most nights, the only thing lacking is a good view. *In the Fairmont Jasper Park Lodge, Old Lodge Rd. ☎ 780/ 852-6052. www.fairmont.com/ jasper. Entrees $24–$39. AE, DC, MC, V. Daily 6–9pm. Map p 126.*

North Face Pizza JASPER *PIZZA* If you want to order in, do so from Jasper's best pizza joint. Free delivery anywhere in town. There are also burgers, salads, pastas, sandwiches, and wings on offer, plus

A dish from the highly regarded Moose's Nook Northern Grill inside the Jasper Park Lodge.

A kid-sized flatbread pizza from the Rocky Mountain Flatbread Company.

locally brewed beer from Big Rock Brewery on tap. Eat in (order at the counter) if you want to mingle with the local under-30 crowd. *618 Connaught Dr.* ☎ *780/852-5830. www. northface.foodpages.ca. Pizzas $9–$22. AE, MC, V. Daily 11am–2am. Map p 126.*

kids Rocky Mountain Flatbread Company CANMORE *MEDITERRANEAN* The wood-fired clay oven here is allegedly the largest in Canada. Handcrafted flatbread pizzas are made with organic flour, regional cheeses, and fresh, creative toppings. The Nemo has prawns, artichokes, and asiago cheese. Salads are big and creative. Pint-sized portions for kids and a kid-friendly play area, where they can bake their own pretend pizzas, are available. *838 10th St.* ☎ *403/609-5508. www.rocky mountainflatbread.ca. Entrees $14–$28. AE, MC, V. Daily 11:30am–10pm. Map p 126.*

★ Syrahs of Jasper JASPER *EUROPEAN* It's the consistency, with quality food and good service, that keeps this spot (formerly known as Andy's Bistro) a top choice in Jasper. The best dishes are traditional Swiss blended with tastes from around the world, like veal emince Zurich-style and filet mignon with pesto and goat cheese. Portions are very large. There's an accessible wine list. *606 Patricia St.* ☎ *780/852-4559. www.syrahsjasper.com. Reservations recommended. Entrees $19–$37. AE, MC, V. Daily 5–11pm. Map p 126.*

★★ Tekarra Restaurant JASPER *INTERNATIONAL* This little cabin inside the sprawling lodge of the same name draws Jasper's keenest foodies. The menu spans from locally sourced ingredients like bison and Alberta beef to venison and Arctic char, always with a creative flair that's both rustic and refined. All the smoking, curing, and baking is done in house. Open only from late May to early October. *In Tekarra Lodge, Hwy. 93A 1km (.62 miles) south of Jasper Townsite.* ☎ *780/852-4624. www.tekarra restaurant.com. Reservations recommended. Entrees $29–$45. MC, V. Daily 5:30–10pm. Map p. 126.*

★★★ The Trough Dining Co. CANMORE *BISTRO* With a relaxed and intimate vibe, this is Canmore's top restaurant. Flavors are powerful and intense in every dish. Labor-intensive entrees include jerk-spiced Alberta baby back ribs and scallops with pork belly, both chock full of fresh ingredients and surprising tastes. The staff is highly professional and the wine list is extensive. If you're on a budget, come for just a glass of wine and dessert. *725 9th St., behind Main St. btw. 6th and 7th aves.* ☎ *403/678-2820. www. thetrough.ca. Reservations highly recommended. Entrees $35–$39. AE, MC, V. Wed–Mon 5:30–10pm. Map p 126.*

One of the rustic cottages at Alpine Village.

Accommodations
Alpine Club of Canada Clubhouse CANMORE
The national headquarters for Canada's Alpine Club is just outside Canmore and houses a sweet hostel-style inn. It's a budget-friendly choice and a hub for meeting fellow hikers, skiers, and adventurers. There's a kitchen, barbecues, laundry, and a great view. *201 Indian Flats Rd.* ☎ *403/678-3200. www.alpineclubofcanada.ca. 12 units. $25 for club members, $35 for nonmembers. MC, V. Map p 126.*

★★ Alpine Village JASPER
On the banks of the rushing Athabasca River, these rustic yet stylish log cottages make a cozy, romantic base, good for simply enjoying the natural beauty of the park. They range from brand-new deluxe bedroom suites to quaint cabins dating back to 1941. All have some form of a kitchenette. Cabins farthest from the road are quieter, but those along the river (next to the road) have the best views. *2.5km (1½ miles) south of Jasper Townsite on the Icefields Pkwy., Hwy. 93, at the junction with Hwy. 93A.* ☎ *780/852-3285. www.alpinevillagejasper.com. 41 units, 28 with kitchenettes. Cabins $180–$490. MC, V. Closed mid-Oct to end of April. Map p 126.*

Blackstone Mountain Lodge CANMORE
Settle into your own condo at this vacation rental property. The decor is urban chic, but the views are definitely all natural. Fully equipped units have one, two, or three bedrooms, private balconies, granite countertops, stainless steel appliances, and even a wine cabinet. A good base if you're

The urban decor at Blackstone Mountain Lodge.

A public area inside the historic Fairmont Jasper Park Lodge.

coming for a week or more. *170 Kananaskis Way.* ☎ *888/830-8883 or 403/609-8098. www.black stonecanmore.ca. 123 units. Weekly rates $1,169–$1,540. AE, MC, V. Map p 126.*

Delta Lodge at Kananaskis

KANANASKIS COUNTRY   The premier hotel in "K-Country" sits at the heart of the multisport village, with a shopping arcade, restaurants, and trails at your doorstep. It's a big place and typically hosts conferences (it hosted the G8 Leaders Summit in 2002). The Signature Club rooms are more private and include breakfast. Great spot for golfers. *1 Centennial Dr., Kananaskis Village.* ☎ *800/268-1111 or 403/591-7711. www.deltalodgeatkananaskis.ca. 321 units. Doubles $229–$324. AE, DC, MC, V. Map p 126.*

★★★ Fairmont Jasper Park Lodge Built in 1923, this historic lodge epitomizes the pampered wilderness experience. It's like an upscale summer camp for adults spread over the largest commercial property in the Canadian Rockies

(with a revered golf course, gorgeous lake, stables, and outdoor pool). The guest rooms are mostly in single-story cabins and cottages spread throughout the property. A new spa opened in late 2010. Ask about packages and promotions. *4km (2½ miles) east of Jasper on Hwy. 16, 3.2km (2 miles) southeast of Maligne Lake Rd.* ☎ *800/441-1414 or 780/852-3301. Fax 780/852-5107. www.fairmont.com/jasper. 446 units. Doubles $349–$399. AE, DC, DISC, MC, V. Map p 126.*

Jasper International Hostel

JASPER   This is the best choice for budget travelers in Jasper, but it's best if you have a car. There are two dorms that are very big, where you'll sleep in bunk beds. Bathrooms are all shared. Family rooms are also available. The shared kitchen is very handy. There is a fun full-time activity program that will get you out exploring Jasper. *4km (2½ miles) south of Jasper Townsite on Hwy. 93, turn west on Tramway Rd. and follow for 3km (1¾ miles).* ☎ *877/852-0781 or 780/852-3215. www.hihostels.ca.*

The cozy Paintbox Lodge.

5 units (2 dormitory-style rooms, 3 private family rooms), 84 beds total. Private doubles $73; dorm beds $30. MC, V. Map p 126.

Mt. Edith Cavell Hostel JASPER
This simple and remote shelter is a good base for backpackers and hikers. It sleeps 32 people in two cabins. It also has no electricity or flush toilets, but there's a self-catering kitchen and awe-inspiring scenery all around. Private doubles are available. Members of Hostelling International receive a discount. Open mid-June to mid-October only. *On Cavell Rd.; take Hwy. 93A south from the townsite to Cavell Rd.; turn west and continue for 13km/8 miles to the hostel, on the east side of the road.* ☎ 866/762-4122 or 780/852-3215. *www.hihostels.ca. 32 beds. Shared dorm $26.50. MC, V. Map p 126.*

★★ Paintbox Lodge CANMORE
A winner for its cozy vibe, friendly service, and location (just steps from Main St.), this is Canmore's best boutique-style inn. The eight guest rooms are all different and all comfortable; upstairs ones have high ceilings with a cozy sitting area. The two-bedroom suite is good for families. *629 10th St.* ☎ 888/678-6100 or 403/609-0482. *www.paintboxlodge.com. 5 units.*

Doubles $210–$259. AE, MC, V. Map p 126.

★★ Park Place Inn JASPER
This is the only place in town one could call an upscale boutique inn, with reasonable rates to boot. The 12 spacious rooms have a cowboy heritage theme, with beautiful linens, goose-down duvets, hardwood floors, huge tubs (many are claw-foot style), and plenty of space. Located upstairs on the bustling Patricia Street, it feels downtown (if that's possible in Jasper). *623 Patricia St.* ☎ 866/852-9770 or 780/852-9770. *www.parkplaceinn.com. 14 rooms. Doubles $229–$269. AE, MC, V. Map p 126.*

Pine Bungalows JASPER
Cabins ensconced along the Athabasca River are nostalgic and family-friendly. Most of them have fireplaces, and nearly all of them have kitchenettes. The best cabins are nos. 1 through 12, right on the river. A good choice if you don't need to be pampered and want your privacy. Open May through early October. *Just off Hwy. 16 and the Jasper Townsite turnoff.* ☎ 780/852-3491. *www.pinebungalows.com. 72 cabins, 57 with kitchens; 25 motel rooms. Cabins $150–$210. AE, MC, V. Map p 126.*

Pyramid Lake Resort JASPER
With a picturesque lakeside setting, this small resort offers plenty of activities, solitude, and lovely new rooms. Walls are thin. The top-floor Cavell Rooms, built in the late 1990s, are the largest and most modern guest rooms, perfect for families planning on staying a few days. It's slow-paced up here and you'll need a car. *6km (3¾ miles) north from Jasper Townsite on Pyramid Lake Rd.* ☎ 888/852-7737 or 780/852-4900. *www.mpljasper.com. 62 units. Doubles $259–$409. AE, DC, MC, V. Map p 126.*

A tent site at Whistlers Campground.

Wapiti Campground JASPER

This is the only campground in the park that's open year-round, and in summer it's quieter than Whistlers. There are 362 sites, 322 of which are for tents only. More than a third of the sites remain accessible in winter. There are often elk roaming about here—remember to keep your distance. *4km (2½ miles) south of Jasper Townsite on the Icefields Pkwy., Hwy. 93, on the east side. Summer: 362 sites, 40 with electrical hookup. $27 tents; $32 RVs. Open Victoria Day long weekend (late May) and mid-June to early Sept. Winter: 93 sites, 40 with electrical hookup. $18 tents; $22 RVs. Open early Oct to early May. Map p 126.*

Whistlers Campground JASPER

This is the biggest campground in Jasper, with 781 sites. It's also just south of town, on the Icefields Parkway (Hwy. 93). It can feel busy and noisy. There are fun interpretive programs put on in the summer evenings. Of the 177 RV sites, 100 have electrical hookups only; the other 77 sites have full hookups. I've twice seen a bear here—so keep your food stored properly. *3km (1¾ miles) south of Jasper Townsite on the Icefields Pkwy., Hwy. 93, on the west side. 781 sites, 100 with electrical hookup only, 77 with full hookup. $23–$27 tents; $32 electrical hookup; $38 full hookup. Open early May to early Oct. Map p 126.*

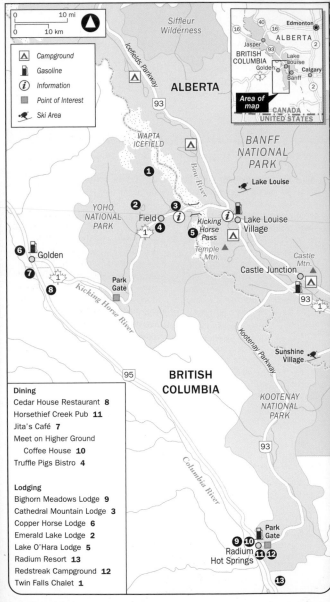

BC Rockies **Dining & Lodging**

Dining

Cedar House Restaurant **8**
Horsethief Creek Pub **11**
Jita's Café **7**
Meet on Higher Ground
   Coffee House **10**
Truffle Pigs Bistro **4**

Lodging

Bighorn Meadows Lodge **9**
Cathedral Mountain Lodge **3**
Copper Horse Lodge **6**
Emerald Lake Lodge **2**
Lake O'Hara Lodge **5**
Radium Resort **13**
Redstreak Campground **12**
Twin Falls Chalet **1**

Dining & Lodging A to Z

Restaurants

★★ Cedar House Restaurant

GOLDEN *CANADIAN* Fresh and inspired food in a rural setting, the passionate chefs here offer simple and local ingredients, creating entrees like tamarind free-range chicken breast, slow-braised lamb shank, and a spectacular espresso and maple syrup buffalo steak. Meats are all natural, and the fish is wild. For dessert, there are homemade sorbets. *735 Hefti Rd. ☎ 250/344-4679. www.cedarhousechalets. com. Entrees $23–$35. MC, V. Reservations recommended. Wed–Sun 5–9pm. Map p 134.*

Horsethief Creek Pub RADIUM

PUB The menu here is almost as expansive as the views across the Columbia Valley. The famous half-pound burger comes with mushrooms, bacon, and melted cheese. Pasta lovers will be tempted by Kootenai curry fettuccini or Louisiana prawn penne. It's also a nice spot for an afternoon beer and nibbles. *7538 Main St. ☎ 250/347-6400. www.horsethiefpub.ca. Entrees*

$12–$26. MC, V. Summer daily noon–10pm; winter closed Mon–Tues. Pub open weekends until midnight. Map p 134.*

Jita's Café GOLDEN *CAFE* For a

healthy meal or a midafternoon coffee break, head to this funky cafe in downtown Golden. Besides baked goods that are served fresh out of the oven, there are soups, sandwiches, and salads. I particularly like the Thai Asian salad. *B–1007 11th St. ☎ 250/344-3660. Sandwiches $6–$12. No credit cards. Tues–Sat 8am–6pm. Map p 134.*

Meet on Higher Ground Coffee House RADIUM *CAFE* The options

in Radium aren't great, but this cozy cafe has by far the best coffee and baked goods in the village. Breakfast bagels and hearty sandwiches make for good picnics. *7527 Main St., Ste. 6. ☎ 250/347-6567. www. meetonhigherground.com. Breakfast and sandwiches $5–$12. MC, V. Daily 6am–5pm. Map p 134.*

★★ Truffle Pigs Bistro FIELD

CAFE Field took center stage for

A burger from the Horsethief Creek Pub.

Field's Truffle Pigs Bistro.

foodies when this cafe became a bistro and moved across the street. The chef offers options like coconut curry ragout and an unforgettable lamb and fig sandwich. Handmade desserts and a good wine list make it the best stop between Lake Louise and Golden. *100 Centre St.* ☎ *250/343-6303. www.trufflepigs. com. Lunch $9–$21; dinner entrees $18–$36. MC, V. Summer daily 7–10:30am; winter 11am–9pm. Map p 134.*

Accommodations
Bighorn Meadows Lodge

RADIUM At last something besides a motel in Radium. These are vacation rentals at a new condo

Cathedral Mountain Lodge's "Grand Room."

development on the west side of town. They're new, so they're clean and have great views. Units have private balconies with barbecues overlooking the golf course. Guest rooms are a bargain but don't have kitchens. *10 Bighorn Blvd., Radium Hot Springs, BC.* ☎ *877/344-2323 or 250/347-2323. www.bighorn meadows.ca. 96 units. Apartments $139–$379. AE, MC, V. Map p 134.*

★★ Cathedral Mountain Lodge

FIELD If it's a cozy log cabin in a peaceful and powerful setting you're after, this is an excellent choice. This lodge offers a beautiful blend of privacy and luxury tucked beneath its namesake mountain along the banks of the glacier-fed Kicking Horse River. Quintessential cabins are functional and cute (if somewhat close together), with fireplaces, modern bathtubs, and fluffy duvets. *Take the Trans-Canada Hwy. 5km (3 miles) west from the Alberta–British Columbia border or 2km (1¼ miles) east of Field, BC, and turn northwest on Yoho Valley Rd.; continue 4km (2½ miles) to lodge.* ☎ *866/619-6442 or 250/343-6442. www.cathedralmountainlodge.com. 31 units. Cabins $289–$439. AE, MC, V. Map p 134.*

Copper Horse Lodge GOLDEN
At the base of Kicking Horse Mountain Resort, this boutique-size inn has a stylish mountain vibe, lovely service, and a supremely relaxing feel. Built only a few years ago, it's a good choice if your aim is to rip it up at the resort or find some quiet romance. Otherwise, it's out of the way. *At end of Kicking Horse Mtn. Rd.; turn right after the gondolas.* ☎ *877/544-7644 or 250/344-7644. www.copperhorselodge.com. 10 units. Doubles $195–$245. MC, V. Map p 134.*

★ **Emerald Lake Lodge** FIELD
This luxurious but cozy lodge, made up of 24 buildings on a 5-hectare (12 acres) peninsula in the heart of Yoho National Park is splendid. Each guest room has a fieldstone fireplace and warm, rustic decor, including dark green marble vanities in many bathrooms (although others remain in need of a face-lift). Most rooms have a balcony. The real star, however, is Emerald Lake itself, a glow of turquoise that never escapes the corner of your eye. *1 Emerald Lake Road, Field, BC. Take Trans-Canada Hwy. 2km* (1¼ miles) *south of Field to Emerald Lake Rd. turnoff; continue 8km* (5 miles). ☎ *800/663-6336 or 250/343-6321. www.crmr.com. 85 units. Doubles $315–$1,000. AE, MC, V. Map p 134.*

★★★ **Lake O'Hara Lodge** YOHO NATIONAL PARK In a secluded alpine valley, there are no phones, no television, no roads, and no cars here (see the box "Getting to Lake O'Hara," p 108). This is a paradise that is one of a kind. Cabins have comfortable beds and modern bathrooms; meals are included. It's a wonderful getaway for city slickers and a true mecca for mountain lovers of all ages. Reserve well in advance. *Access via the Parks Canada bus that leaves the Lake O'Hara parking lot.* ☎ *250/343-6418, June–Sept.* ☎ *is 403/678-4110, Oct–May. www.lakeohara.com. 8 lodge rooms, 8 cabins. Rates include all meals, tips, taxes, and bus transportation. Doubles $460–$865. No credit cards. Map p 134.*

Radium Resort RADIUM HOT SPRINGS This relaxed four-season resort is primarily for golfers.

A room inside the Copper Horse Lodge.

A room inside the Emerald Lake Lodge.

Accommodations are moderately priced. The rooms are all large, and most have excellent views and large balconies. The two-level lofts are great for families and groups. *4km (2½ miles) south of Radium on Hwy. 93/95, east side.* ☎ *800/667-6444 or 250/347-9311. Fax 250/347-6299. www.radiumresort.com. 90 units. Doubles $149–$199. AE, MC, V. Map p 134.*

One of the cabin's at Lake O'Hara Lodge.

Redstreak Campground

RADIUM HOT SPRINGS   There's lots to do at Parks Canada's largest campground in Kootenay National Park, including nightly entertainment in the summer and a network of trails heading into the park. It's located behind the Visitors Centre. Reserve a campsite online at www. pccamping.ca or call ☎ 877/737-3783. *2.5km (1½ miles) southwest of Radium Hot Springs, turn east off Hwy. 93 at the sign.* ☎ *250/347-9505. 242 sites, 38 with electrical hookup only, 50 with full hookup. $27–$38. AE, MC, V. Open May 11– Oct 8. Map p 134.*

Twin Falls Chalet YOHO

NATIONAL PARK   Tucked beneath one of the loveliest waterfalls in Yoho (and the competition is fierce!), this historic log cabin was built in 1908 and offers simple, rustic backcountry lodging for hikers. There is no electricity, although solar panels keep things warm and bright. *In Yoho Valley. Reserve by telephone only at* ☎ *403/228-7079. 15 beds. $250 per person, 2-night minimum, includes all meals. No credit cards. Open late June to mid-Sept. Map p 134.* ●

6 The Great Outdoors

The Best **Hiking in Banff**

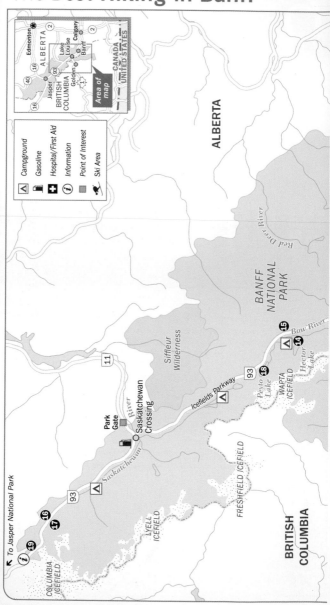

Previous Page: Canoeing on the Bow River.

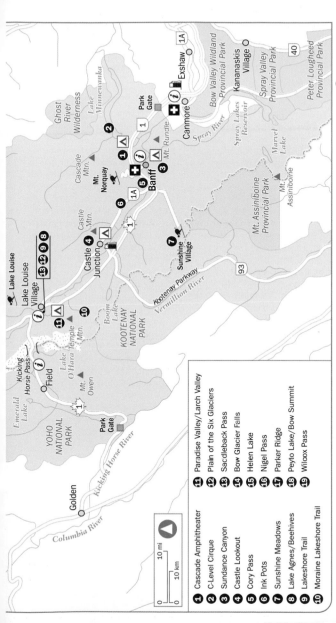

1 Cascade Amphitheater
2 C-Level Cirque
3 Sundance Canyon
4 Castle Lookout
5 Cory Pass
6 Ink Pots
7 Sunshine Meadows
8 Lake Agnes/Beehives
9 Lakeshore Trail
10 Moraine Lakeshore Trail
11 Paradise Valley/Larch Valley
12 Plain of the Six Glaciers
13 Sacdleback Pass
14 Bow Glacier Falls
15 Helen Lake
16 Nigel Pass
17 Parker Ridge
18 Peyto Lake/Bow Summit
19 Wilcox Pass

0   10 mi
0   10 km

The hiking season in Banff usually gets started in mid-June and winds down in October. Trails on the southern slopes and at lower elevations are free of snow earlier in the season and open earlier. In spring, trails are often extremely wet and muddy. In autumn, many days are sunny and warm, but the variability of the weather poses a new challenge, since snow may begin to accumulate over high passes.

Town of Banff Hikes

★ **Cascade Amphitheater.** You can't miss Cascade Mountain—the beautiful pyramid-shaped peak at the northeastern end of Banff Avenue. One of the most rewarding day hikes in the townsite area, this is a demanding outing that starts (and later finishes) at the Mt. Norquay day lodge and takes you into a high alpine cirque in a hanging valley with a lush carpet of subalpine wildflowers. The trail crests at a dramatic point on the south edge of the meadows, on a small knoll of rockslide debris. *7.7km (4.8 miles) each way. Strenuous. Elevation gain is 640m (2,100 ft.). 6 hr. round-trip. Trail head is Mt. Norquay ski area. Map p 140.*

★ **C-Level Cirque.** This trail has wonderful panoramic views and is a great afternoon getaway from busy Banff Avenue. After alighting on a stunning view of Lake Minnewanka, the trail heads back into the now-subalpine forest before ending in a small cirque (like a bowl with a circular ridge surrounding it) at the highest part of the valley. Look for calypso orchids, marmots, and pika as you climb to the treeless alpine zone. *3.9km (2.4 miles) each way. Moderate. Elevation gain 455m (1,493 ft.). 3 hr. round-trip. Trail head is Upper Bankhead picnic area parking lot, 3.5km (2¼ miles) on Minnewanka Rd. from the Minnewanka interchange on the Trans-Canada Hwy. Map p 140.*

kids Sundance Canyon. A gentle hike that leaves from the Cave and Basin Historic Site is good in spring and fall. There are nice views of the Sawback Range and the pinnacle of Mt. Edith. It goes up a paved trail, turning at Sundance Creek and continuing on to an extraordinary canyon with giant boulders. Head over the bridge and up the stairs for the best views. *4.3km (2.7 miles) each way. Easy. Elevation gain 143m (469 ft.). 3 hr. round-trip. Trail head at Cave and Basin Historic Site. Map p 140.*

Bow Valley Parkway & Sunshine Meadows

Castle Lookout. This hike gets you close to a former fire lookout on this scenic mountain. Short but steep, the trail offers an amazing panorama of the glacier-chiseled Bow Valley and Storm Mountain, which is often surrounded by its own gnarly

A hiker at Cory Pass.

Easy to Hard: Difficulty Ratings

Hiking times depend on a hiker's experience and fitness, as well as the weather conditions. Hikers of an average fitness level can usually hike 2.5 to 3.5km (1.6–2.2 miles) in an hour. Steeper trails will take longer, and you'll want to add in time for lunch, snack, and rest breaks.

Easy: Hikes that are generally smooth and gentle, usually less than 6km (3.7 miles) long with an elevation gain of no more than 300m (984 ft.).

Moderate: Hikes up to 13km (8 miles) long on well-established trails with some exposure. Elevation gain can be up to 600m (1,969 ft.).

Difficult: Hikes longer than 13km (8 miles), with an elevation gain of more than 600m (1,969 ft.). Often on poorly defined trails, with obstacles and exposed terrain.

Lengths listed here are total distance from the start to the finish of the hikes. Elevation gain is the total ascent from the lowest point on the trail to the highest point.

weather system. This trail can be very warm on a sunny day and is a great "shoulder season" choice. *3.7km (2.3 miles) each way. Strenuous. Elevation gain 520m (1,706 ft.). 3–4 hr. round-trip. Trail head is parking lot on the north side of the Bow Valley Pkwy. 1A, 5km (3 miles) west of Castle Junction. Map p 140.*

★ **Cory Pass.** This is one of the most strenuous and challenging hikes in Banff, but it's also by far the most spectacular one near the Town of Banff. The highlight is the 2,300m (7,546-ft.) monolithic limestone cliffs of the Sawback Range. The trail starts in a high, subalpine valley bottom and ends in a high alpine zone well above the tree line—tremendous ecological diversity. Be sure to take a good map with you on this trail (see sidebar on p 145). *5.8km (3.6 miles) each way. Very strenuous. Elevation gain is 915m (3,002 ft.). 6–7 hr. round-trip. Trail head is Fireside Picnic Area at the eastern end of the Bow Valley Pkwy. 1A. Map p 140.*

Ink Pots. Continue past the crowds at Johnston Canyon, passing the Upper Falls, twice the size of the lower ones. The trail opens into a lovely, wide valley and takes you to jade-colored natural springs. It's a magical place and very quiet after the rush of the canyon. *5.5km (3.4 miles) each way. Moderate. Elevation gain 243m (797 ft.). 4–5 hr. round-trip. Trail head is Johnston Canyon parking lot, 18km (11 miles) west of Banff on the Bow Valley Pkwy. 1A. Map p 140.*

★★ **kids Sunshine Meadows.** Located high in an alpine bowl that is also the site of the Sunshine Village ski resort in winter, this alpine meadow is famous for its annual display of beautiful wildflowers and is incredibly easy to get to—just take a shuttle to the Sunshine Village day lodge, where all trail heads are located. **White Mountain Adventures** (☎ 800/408-0005 or 403/762-7889; www.sunshine meadowsbanff.com) runs a shuttle service to the area.

You'll find beautiful alpine views at Sunshine Meadows.

The Rock Isle Lake trail leads you to the other side of the Continental Divide, into British Columbia's Mt. Assiniboine Provincial Park. Rock Lake is particularly lovely in the calm early morning, when it mirrors the surrounding scenery, and the view stretches off into British Columbia's mountains. It's a favorite of artists and photographers.

The Simpson Pass/Healy Meadows trail is worth an afternoon outing for rewarding views of Wawa Ridge, Mt. Assiniboine, and the Monarch, a massive pyramid-shaped peak. It's a wildflower lover's dream, and a favorite of Banff's old outfitters and pioneers, including Jim Brewster and "Wild Bill" Peyto, two of Banff's original mountain guides. *Rock Isle Lake trail: 2.5km (1.6 miles) each way. Easy. Elevation gain is 105m (344 ft.). 2 hr. round-trip. Map p 140. Simpson Pass/Healy Meadows: 7.6km (4.7 miles) each way. Moderate. Elevation gain is 160m (525 ft.). 5 hr. round-trip. Map p 140.*

Lake Louise Hikes

★★ Lake Agnes/Beehives. In a picturesque hanging valley above Lake Louise, Lake Agnes has been a favorite for more than a century. There are great views of the Bow Valley and wonderful history to be had at the Lake Agnes Teahouse on the shore of the lake, which serves freshly baked scones and tea throughout the summer. From the teahouse, take the trail to the north shore of the lake to connect with the Big Beehive. *5.1km (3.2 miles) each way. Moderate. Elevation gain is 400m (1,312 ft.). 4 hr. round-trip. Trail head is Lake Louise shoreline trail, in front of the Fairmont Chateau Lake Louise. Map p 140.*

kids Lakeshore Trail. This broad, flat trail may be among the most well-trodden paths in Banff National Park. It leads you away from the crowds, around the north shore of the lake to

The Lake Agnes Teahouse.

Hiking To-Do List

1. **Select a trail.** Read through the hikes listed here, pick up a map and other hiking guides, and chat with the staff at the Banff Information Centre (224 Banff Ave.; ☎ 403/763-1550; www.pc.gc.ca/banff) or the Lake Louise Visitors Centre (Samson Mall, 101 Lake Louise Dr.; ☎ 403/522-3833) to get the right trail for you.

2. **Get a map.** The best are topographic maps, with a scale of 1:50,000. The Canadian government produces maps with lots of detail, but they are short on hiking trails. GemTrek Maps produces the best hiking maps in the Canadian Rockies. Pick one up in Banff or order at www.gemtrek.com. They're waterproof, tear-resistant, and have topographic contours, key for measuring elevation changes.

3. **Check the weather.** Get the up-to-date forecast by calling Banff National Park (☎ 403/762-1550) or Environment Canada in Banff at ☎ 403/762-2088.

4. **Check trail conditions.** Call the Park at ☎ 403/762-1550 for the latest trail reports, which are also posted around town and online at www.pc.gc.ca/banff. And be sure to find out about any bear warnings and area closures due to bear activity.

5. **Bring plenty of water.** At least 1 liter (2 pints) of water per person, more if you're going on a strenuous full-day hike.

6. **Go in a group.** Some areas of Banff are under bear warnings and hikers must stay in groups of four or six at a time. It's safer and often more fun!

7. **Tell someone about it.** Let someone know where you're going and when you'll be back.

the base of Mt. Victoria and the shimmering Victoria Glacier. There are many benches along the trail where you can sit and marvel at Lake Louise's color and beauty. Come early in the morning to beat the crowds. *1.9km (1.2 miles) each way. Easy. No elevation gain. 1 hr. round-trip. Trail head is in front of Fairmont Chateau Lake Louise. Map p 140.*

Moraine Lakeshore Trail.

Moraine Lake is a popular destination, but luckily this trail, along the western shore of the lake, is still a peaceful and pleasant way to enjoy the dramatic and imposing Valley of the Ten Peaks. The best views are at

the start of the trail, but for a spectacular view of Moraine Lake at the end of the hike head 5 minutes up to the Moraine Lake Viewpoint, at the south end of the parking lot, following the sign to Consolation Lakes. *1.2km (.7 mile) each way. Easy. No elevation gain. 1 hr. round-trip. Trail head is Moraine Lake parking lot. Map p 140.*

★★★ Paradise Valley/Larch Valley. A rewarding and challenging full-day hike, you'll hike below mounts Temple and Lefroy, and past Lake Annette, Horseshoe Meadows, and the "Giant's Staircase" waterfall, then over Sentinel Pass and down

The rushing Paradise Creek in Paradise Valley.

through Larch Valley to Moraine Lake—all superb highlights. The trail ends at a different parking lot from where it begins, so you'll need to organize a shuttle. Parks Canada often requires hikers to stay in groups of six or more due to bear activity in the area. *17km (11 miles) each way. Strenuous. Elevation gain is 880m (2,887 ft.). 6–7 hr. Trail head is 2.5km (1½ miles) south on the Moraine Lake Rd. from Lake Louise Rd., in the Paradise Valley lot, on the right side of the road. Map p 140.*

★★ **Plain of the Six Glaciers.** If you have time for only one half-day hike in Lake Louise, take this route through postcard-worthy scenery as it makes its way around Lake Louise and below mounts Victoria and Lefroy. It empties into a harsh

Hiking through the Plain of the Six Glaciers.

glacier- and avalanche-scoured terrain before climbing into a lush meadow, where you can stop at the historic Plain of the Six Glaciers Teahouse. From the summit of a small moraine, you'll have the glaciers spread out before you. *5.3km (3.3 miles) each way. Moderate. Elevation gain 365m (1,198 ft.). 4–5 hr. round-trip. Trail head is Lake Louise Shoreline trail in front of Fairmont Chateau Lake Louise hotel. Map p 140.*

Saddleback Pass. The trail takes you to a stupendous view of the colossal Mt. Temple from a pass between Saddle and Fairview mountains. Heading out along the lower slopes of Mt. Fairview, the trail switchbacks up to a flower-filled meadow. It's steep, so bring poles to ease the trip down. Continue a bit farther to Fairview's summit for a mile-high view of Lake Louise. *3.7km (2.3 miles) one-way to pass. Moderate to strenuous. Elevation gain is 595m (1,952 ft.). 4 hr. round-trip. Trail head is on the south shore of Lake Louise to the right of the old guide's cabin. Map p 140.*

Icefields Parkway Hikes
kids Bow Glacier Falls. When the Bow Glacier retreated, it left behind a majestic 120m (394-ft.) waterfall that simply hints at the massive icefield above it. The trail is broad and scenic alongside the flats skirting Bow Lake, a Rocky Mountain

gem. At the western shore of the lake there are views of the stunning Crowfoot and Bow glaciers. Only 100 years ago, the Bow Glacier extended to cover the entire Bow Valley. *4.7km (2.9 miles) each way. Easy. Elevation gain 95m (312 ft.). 3 hr. round-trip. Trail head is beside Num-Ti-Jah Lodge 36km (22 miles) north of the Lake Louise junction on Icefields Pkwy. 93. Map p 140.*

★ **Helen Lake.** With tall peaks, alpine meadows, lakes, and wide views, this trail is diverse enough to draw you enthusiastically around every corner. This is a relatively quick and pain-free way to access the high alpine environment. The lakeside meadows draw friendly hoary marmots. Check out the view of the Crowfoot Glacier. *6km (3.7 miles) each way. Moderate. Elevation gain 455m (1,493 ft.). 4 hr. round-trip. Trail head is across the highway from the Crowfoot Glacier Viewpoint, 33km (21 miles) north of the Lake Louise junction on Icefields Pkwy. 93. Map p 140.*

★ **Nigel Pass.** On this rewarding hike that tops out on a rocky

A hiker crosses a creek at Helen Lake.

2,195m (7,201-ft.) ridge marking the boundary between Banff and Jasper national parks, you'll have great views of the Columbia Icefield. East of the pass, you can scramble over rocks to catch sight of the Brazeau River and the waterfall along the rocky north wall of Nigel Pass. *7.2km (4.5 miles) each way. Moderate. Elevation gain 365m (1,198 ft.). 5 hr. round-trip. Trail head is 2.5km (1½ miles) north of the "Big Bend" switchback (114km/71 miles north of the Lake Louise junction) or 8.5km (5¼ miles) south of the Banff–Jasper*

Traveling Safely in Bear Country

Banff National Park is home to both black and grizzly bears. You could see a bear from your car, from your hotel, or even while out exploring the mountains on foot. Be prepared! Avoid having an encounter with a bear while hiking by making your presence well known so as not to surprise the bear—sing, talk, clap your hands, call "Hey Bear!" every few minutes while you hike, especially in densely forested areas or when crossing avalanche paths. Carry bear spray and know how to use it. And keep your eyes and ears open at all times.

If you see a bear, try not to panic. Speak loudly and firmly to the bear and try to appear large by waving your arms. Back away slowly: Do not run!

For more information, visit www.pc.gc.ca/banff-bears.

Parker Ridge is a direct route to stunning views.

boundary on the Icefields Pkwy. 93. Parking lot is on northeast side of the highway. Map p 140.

★★★ **Parker Ridge.** The best short day hike in the Icefields Parkway area, this high and open trail takes you high up and straight into the heart of the unforgiving alpine zone. In summer—which can last only a few weeks up here—the meadows turn a brilliant red with heather. Once you reach the summit, enjoy views of the Saskatchewan Glacier (the glacier that reaches the farthest out into a valley in the Columbia Icefield) below you. *2.7km (1.7 miles) each way. Moderate. Elevation gain 250m (820 ft.). 3 hr. round-trip. Trail head is in parking lot on the west side of the*

Icefields Pkwy. 93, 4km (2½ miles) south of the Banff–Jasper park boundary. Map p 140.

Peyto Lake/Bow Summit. This is the most popular short hike along the Icefields Parkway. Escape the crowds by continuing on to the Bow Summit lookout; then hike down to the lake for an almost bird's-eye view of the Bow River's source. This trail takes you through what is known as the transition zone; what begins as a thick forest soon becomes a stunted one, getting sparser and sparser until you come to an area where there isn't a single tree growing. *3.1km (1.9 miles) each way. Easy. Elevation gain 230m (755 ft.). 2 hr. round-trip. Trail head is Bow Summit parking lot, 41km (25 miles) north of the Lake Louise junction on Icefields Pkwy. 93. Map p 140.*

★★★ **Wilcox Pass** Starting just across the border in Jasper National Park, this trail gives you an almost bird's-eye view of the spectacular Columbia Icefield from the edge of a gorgeous alpine valley. It's an incredibly rewarding—albeit popular—trail since it's mostly above the tree line, offering nearly nonstop views and plenty of wildflowers in August. *12km (7.4 miles) return. Moderate. Elevation gain 335m (1,099 ft.). 5 hr. round-trip. Trail*

A hiker pauses at Wilcox Pass, looking at the Columbia Icefield.

Backpacking: The Ultimate Rocky Mountain Experience

It's a challenging undertaking—most people just starting to backpack will find the routes in Banff National Park demanding, because of the mountainous terrain. And you must be very well organized with what you bring on the trip. But a night under the stars in the Banff backcountry promises the ultimate Rocky Mountain high. The peak hiking season is from early July to mid-September, and be sure to reserve your campsites ahead of time. There are dozens of possible trips, but the three listed below are my favorites!

head is 2.5km (1.6 miles) south of the Icefields Centre on Icefields Pkwy. 93 at the Wilcox Pass campground. Map p 140.

Backpacking Hikes
★★ Egypt Lake/Shadow Lake.
This is the most popular backpacking area in Banff National Park, a multi-day exploration of Banff's highest-elevation hiking routes. With a series of passes along the Continental Divide, encompassing cliffs, meadows, and lake-dotted alpine cirques, this trail takes you through some quintessential Canadian Rockies landscape. *40km (25 miles) return. Moderate. Elevation gain 790m (2,592 ft.). 2–3 days. Trail head is Sunshine Village ski area. Map p 140.*

kids **Glacier Lake.** This overnight trip isn't too strenuous and gets you into the Icefields Parkway backcountry. It's a nice outing for families, since the hike is quite flat and the elevation is relatively low. The beginning elevation is 1,450m (4,757 ft.) and you gain 210m (689 ft.) over the course of the trip. *8.9km (5.5 miles) each way. Easy. Elevation gain 210m (689 ft.). 2 days. Trail head is on west side of Icefields Pkwy. 93, 1.2km (¾ mile) north of the junction with Hwy. 11, near Saskatchewan Crossing. Map p 140.*

★★★ Sunshine Meadows/Mt. Assiniboine.
Showcasing the spectacularly colorful Sunshine Meadows and Mt. Assiniboine region, this route covers high alpine terrain, crosses dramatic passes, and runs alongside picturesque lakes. Head over Citadel Pass to admire Mt. Assiniboine (the highest mountain in Banff National Park, also known as the "Matterhorn of the Rockies"), in British Columbia's Mt. Assiniboine Provincial Park. *62km (39 miles) return. Moderate to strenuous. Elevation gain 655m (2,149 ft.). 3–6 days. Trail head is Sunshine Village ski area. Map p 140.*

Mount Assiniboine is known as the "Matterhorn of the Rockies."

Summer Sports

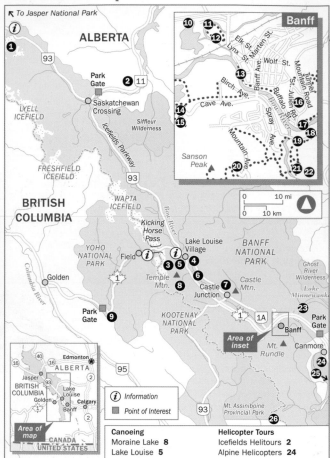

↖ To Jasper National Park

ALBERTA

93

Banff

Park Gate ❷ 11

Saskatchewan Crossing

LYELL ICEFIELD

Siffleur Wilderness

Icefields Parkway

93

FRESHFIELD ICEFIELD

BRITISH COLUMBIA

WAPTA ICEFIELD

Kicking Horse Pass

Bow River

YOHO NATIONAL PARK

Field ⓘ ⓘ ❸ ❹ Lake Louise Village

Temple Mtn. ❻ ❽

Golden

Columbia River

1

Castle Junction ❼ *Castle Mtn.*

BANFF NATIONAL PARK

Ghost River Wilderness

Lake Minnewanka

Park Gate ❾

KOOTENAY NATIONAL PARK

1 1A ❷❸ Park Gate

Banff

Area of inset

Mt. Rundle

Canmore ❷❹ ❷❺

Mt. Assiniboine Provincial Park

93 ❷❻

0 — 10 mi
0 — 10 km

Elk St. Marten St.

Lynx St.

Wolf St. ❿ ⓫ ⓬

Banff Ave.

Buffalo St.

St. Julien Rd.

Tunnel Mountain Road

⓭ Birch Ave.

Cave Ave.

⓮ ⓯

Spray Ave.

St. Julien Rd. ⓰ ⓱ ⓲

Mountain Ave. ⓳

Sanson Peak ⓴ ㉑ ㉒

Area of map

Edmonton ★

16 40

Jasper

16

ALBERTA

93

BRITISH COLUMBIA

2

Lake Louise

Golden

1

Banff

Calgary

2

95

Area of map

CANADA
UNITED STATES

ⓘ Information
■ Point of Interest

Biking
Vermillion Lakes **11**
Banff Springs Golf
   Course drive **18**
Spray River Loop **21**
Bow River Loop **4**

Birdwatching
Cave and Basin
   March **14**
Fenland Trail **12**
Bow River Bridge
   and Castle Junction **7**

Canoeing
Moraine Lake **8**
Lake Louise **5**
Bow River at Banff **13**

Climbing
"Back of the Lake"
   at Lake Louise **3**
Mt Athabasca **1**
Mt Assiniboine **26**

Fishing
Vermillion Lakes **10**
Upper Bow River **6**

Golf
Fairmont Banff
   Springs Golf course **19**

Helicopter Tours
Icefields Helitours **2**
Alpine Helicopters **24**

Horseback Riding
Spray River **22**
Martin Stables **15**

Rafting
Kicking Horse River **9**
Kananaskis River **25**
Bow River **17**

Swimming
Upper Hot Spring **20**
Johnson Lake **23**
Sally Borden Centre **16**

There are many activities to choose from during summer-time in Banff. This isn't a place for loungers. Besides hiking, give yourself a chance to sample a few of the adventures listed below. Get out and try something new!

A mountain biker rides along the Spray River Loop.

Biking

With more than 190km (118 miles) of mountain-bike trails and numerous options for road biking, Banff is a friendly place for two wheels. Bike season runs from May to October. Note that not all hiking trails are open to bikers.

You can rent both road and mountain bikes in Banff National Park at **BacTrax Bike Rentals** (225 Bear St.; ☎ 403/762-8177) and **Adventures Unlimited** (211 Bear St.; ☎ 403/762-4554), which also has kids' bikes, trailers, and strollers. In Lake Louise, rent bikes at **Wilson Mountain Sports** (p 21).

Road Biking Good routes around the Banff Townsite area include the Banff Springs Golf Course drive and the Vermillion Lakes. When you head out from the townsite, take the Bow Valley Parkway (Hwy. 93A).

Share the Trail

Bike trails in Banff National Park are also hiking and horseback-riding trails. Expect to encounter people using the trail in other ways. Ride in control and always be prepared to stop. Slow down when you come upon a hiker. A friendly greeting will make them aware of your presence. Bikes can spook horses: When passing a horse, let the rider know you are coming. If a horse approaches you, move to the side of the trail, stop your bike, and let the horse pass. If you have a chance to stop and chat a little, ask the rider about the trail conditions ahead.

There's much less traffic than on the Trans-Canada Highway (Hwy. 1). If you're up at Lake Louise, try the old Great Divide Road, which leads into Yoho National Park—a quiet ride through mountain scenery.

Mountain Biking Mountain biking is permitted on only a select number of the trails in Banff National Park. You are subject to fines if you are caught biking on hiking-only trails. In the Banff Townsite area, the best ride for beginners and families is the 13km (7.8-mile) Spray River Loop. Near Lake Louise, families with kids will enjoy the relatively flat but very scenic 7.1km (4.4-mile) Bow River Loop, which leaves from the Lake Louise Campground. There are interpretive signs along the trail.

More advanced bikers will find thrills on the steep and narrow Stoney Squaw Loop or along the winding Toe Trail, near the Hoodoos.

Bird-Watching

Birding is a great activity for visitors of all ages. More than 260 species pass through the Canadian Rockies annually. Pick up a brochure from

Climbers take on the "Back of the Lake" route at Lake Louise.

the Banff Information Centre in Banff Townsite (224 Banff Ave.; ☎ 403/762-1550). Great spots close to the Town of Banff include Cave and Basin March and Fenland Trail. Look for an osprey nest on the Bow River Bridge and Castle Junction.

Canoeing

To canoe is to be Canadian, it is said. There are boathouses where you can rent canoes at both Moraine Lake and Lake Louise. The Moraine Lake Lodge's boathouse (14km/8¾ miles south of Lake Louise on Moraine Lake Rd.; ☎ 403/522-3733) rents canoes for $40 per hour. The Fairmont Chateau Lake Louise (111 Lake Louise Dr.; ☎ 403/522-3511) rents canoes for $55 per hour. In the Town of Banff, rent a canoe at the **Blue Canoe-Rentals** (end of Wolf St.; ☎ 403/762-3632) for $36 per hour, where you can paddle straight into the placid Vermillion Lakes.

Be prepared if you're planning on canoeing the Bow River; experience is recommended, particularly in the section between Castle Junction and Banff, where there's a Class III rapid. The paddle from Banff to Canmore is intermediate-level and requires route-finding skills.

Climbing & Mountaineering

Visitors to Banff who've taken the time and energy to learn the ropes enjoy this highly technical sport. There are no specific regulations governing climbing or mountaineering in Banff National Park; however, Parks Canada does suggest you contact the Banff Warden's office (in Banff ☎ 403/762-1470; in Lake Louise ☎ 403/522-1220) for more information before you head out.

There are a number of excellent rock-climbing locations in Banff, including the "Back of the Lake," at Lake Louise. Classic mountain climbs include mounts Athabasca

Fly-fishing on the Bow River.

and Assiniboine—both are for experienced climbers only.

For advice on planning a climbing trip, contact the **Alpine Club of Canada** (☎ 403/678-3200; www.alpine clubofcanada.ca) or the **Association of Canadian Mountain Guides** (☎ 403/678-2885; www.acmg.ca). For private lessons and guiding, contact Canada's premier mountaineering school, **Yamnuska Inc.** (☎ 403/678-4164; www.yamnuska.com).

Fishing

You need a permit to fish in Banff National Park. Pick one up at the Banff Information Centre in Banff Townsite (224 Banff Ave.; ☎ 403/762-1550). National Park fishing permits cost $10 daily. An annual permit costs $34. Vermillion Lakes is a very popular fishing spot, so not surprisingly there aren't too many fish left. Don't even bother trying to fish at Lake Louise—again, there are none left. The Bow River is one of the world's finest fly-fishing rivers and is the only area in Banff National Park open year-round.

Banff Fishing Unlimited (☎ 403/762-4936; www.banff-fishing.com) specializes in year-round fly-fishing, spin casting, and trophy lake-trout fishing. Their guides know all the secrets. **Alpine Anglers** (☎ 403/762-8223; www. alpineanglers.com) offers top-notch instruction in the mild sensibilities of fly-fishing on the pristine, turquoise waters of the Bow River.

Golfing

The Fairmont Banff Springs Hotel's 27-hole **Stanley Thompson Course** is world famous (405 Spray Ave.; ☎ 403/762-6801). Recently upgraded, the course has three tee-offs and an amazingly scenic location along the Spray and Bow rivers, beneath Mt. Rundle. It's expensive but legendary, and open to the public (you don't have to be a guest at the hotel to play a round). Course fees range from $155 in May and October and $225 from June

The Fairmont Banff Springs Hotel and the Banff Springs Golf Course.

Riding horses near Banff.

through September, including cart. There's also a 9-hole course. Watch for geese and elk!

Helicopter Tours

To get the ultimate bird's-eye view of the jaw-droppingly beautiful Rockies, you have to step just outside the boundary of Banff National Park. Near the Icefields Centre, **Icefields Helitours** (☎ 888/844-3514 or 403/721-2100; www.icefieldheli. com) takes those looking to splurge for a thrilling 55-minute chopper ride over the Columbia Icefield

($549 per person). **Alpine Helicopters** (☎ 403/678-4802; www.alpine helicopters.com) takes off just east of Banff in Canmore and flies to Mt. Assiniboine and back in 30 unforgettable minutes ($259 per person). They also have heli-hiking day tours starting at $489.

Horseback Riding

Riding a horse in the Canadian Rockies is as logical as riding a camel in the Sahara Desert. Saddling up not only lets you explore the cowboy heritage of the Rockies, it also lets you wind your way into parts of the Banff backcountry you might not otherwise have seen. Having said this, only a select few trails in Banff National Park are able to accommodate horses, so I recommend taking a trip organized by a local outfitter. They'll show you a good ol' time, while keeping you on course.

    Timberline Tours (☎ 403/522-3743; www.timberlinetours.ca) leads scenic trips at Lake Louise. A half-day outing is between $70 and $149, while overnight trips start at $470. **Holiday on Horseback** (132 Banff Ave., ☎ 800/661-8352 or

Saddle Up & Head High

If you're not sure about long days of hiking and carrying your own packs but you still want to explore the backcountry of Banff, consider an overnight horseback trip. From early May to late October, trail rides range from 1 night to 1 week. Some outfitters combine guided trail rides with stays at rustic but comfortable backcountry lodges, while others include overnights in wilderness tents situated in truly spectacular settings. This is one of the best ways to see the back corners of Banff—with considerably less effort than backpacking. For trips from 2 to 4 days, ranging from $581 to $1,476, try **Holiday on Horseback** (132 Banff Ave.; ☎ 403/762-4551 or 800/661-8352; www.horseback.com). Starting at the Lake Louise Corral, **Timberline Tours** (☎ 403/522-3743; www.timber linetours.ca) has overnight trips starting at $470 per person.

Rafting down the Bow River.

403/762-4551; www.horseback.
com) has a corral at the Fairmont
Banff Springs Hotel, where they run
1-hour tours along the Spray River
($43). They have another corral at
Martin Stables (located on the banks
of the Bow River across from Banff
Townsite), where 5- to 7-hour trips
head into the Sundance Range
($164–$204). They also organize
wonderfully fun wilderness cook-
outs, which include a Mountain

Going for a swim at Johnson Lake.

Morning breakfast ride ($110) and
an Evening Trailride, where they
serve a large Western barbecue dinner ($110). All prices are per person.

Rafting

The gnarliest rapids in the Canadian
Rockies are west of Banff on the
Kicking Horse River (p 111) and east
of Banff on the Kananaskis River.
From the Town of Banff, you can
hop on a gentle float trip down the
Bow River. It's great for families.
Rocky Mountain Raft Tours
(☎ 403/762-3632; www.banffraft
tours.com) departs from just below
Bow Falls and drops you at Canmore for $85 for adults, $40 for
youth 15 and under.

Swimming

The spring-fed outdoor pools at the
historic Banff Upper Hot Springs (p 5)
make for a memorable dip any time
of year. On a hot summer day, join
the locals for an afternoon swim at
Johnson Lake on the Minnewanka
Loop. Throughout the year, the nicest
indoor pool in Banff is at the sunny
Banff Centre's **Sally Borden Centre**
(St. Julien Rd., ☎ 403/762-6450).

Winter Sports

Lake Louise

BANFF NATIONAL PARK

1A
93
1A
1

Lake Louise Dr.

Banff

Elk St.
Lynx St.
St. Marten St.
Wolf St.
Banff Ave.
Birch Ave.
Buffalo St.
St. Julien Rd.
Mountain Road
Tunnel
Cave Ave.
Spray Ave.
Bear St.
Mountain Ave.

Sanson Peak

93

Lake Louise Village

Lake Louise

Area of Lake Louise inset

Bow Valley Parkway

Moraine Lake

Boom Lake

93

KOOTENAY NATIONAL PARK

Kootenay Parkway

Castle Mtn.

Castle Junction

Redearth Creek

Isabelle Pk.

BANFF NATIONAL PARK

Cascade Mtn.

Mt. Norquay

Ghost River Wilderness

Lake Minnewanka

1A

Banff

Area of Banff inset

Sunshine Village

BRITISH COLUMBIA

Simpson River

93

ALBERTA

Mt. Rundle

Park Gate

Canmore

Spray River

Spray Lakes Reservoir

Mt. Assiniboine Provincial Park

Mt. Assiniboine

Marvel Lake

Symbol	Legend
▲	Campground
⛽	Gasoline
✚	Hospital/First Aid
ⓘ	Information
■	Point of Interest
⛷	Ski Area

0   5 mi
0   5 km

Alpine Skiing
Lake Louise Resort **1**
Mt. Norquay **13**
Sunshine Village **14**

Cross-Country Skiing
Golf Course Trail/
   Spray River Loop **9**
Moraine Lake Road **10**
Pipestone **2**

Dog-Sledding
Spray Lakes **16**
Divide Road **3**

Ice Climbing
Yamnuska Inc. **15**

Ice-Skating
Vermillion Lakes **7**
Fairmont Banff
   Springs Hotel **8**

Lake Louise **4**

Ice Walks
Johnston Canyon **12**

Snowshoeing
Fenland Trail **6**
Moose Meadows **11**
Fairview Lookout **5**

Winter is breathtaking in the Canadian Rockies, in both beauty and temperature. Days can drop to −15 °C (5 °F) or lower, but you'll be too busy sampling the many adventures available—some you may have never experienced before—to care. Dress warmly, keep a pair of gloves nearby, and make the most of the sunny days and starry nights.

Alpine Skiing

Lake Louise Resort. The views here will have you picking your jaw up off the glistening powder snow. Easy to access and full of varied terrain, Louise keeps folks loyal. Beginners will find a friendly ski- and snowboard school, as well as some lovely green runs to get started. Head straight to the top of the new Grizzly Express Gondola for more advanced blue runs. Larch is a great place for intermediates. Expert skiers should take to the Top of the World "Six-Pack" Chair and then the Summit Platter and enjoy powder bowls like West Bowl and Boomerang. For snowboarders, there is a terrain park with jumps, obstacles, and railings. Cozy and rustic Temple Lodge, tucked in behind the resort below Whitehorn Mountain, is a good lunch restaurant. *Follow Whitehorn Rd. off the Trans-Canada Hwy. 1 at the Lake Louise exit.* ☎ *800/258-7669 or 403/522-3555. www.skilouise.com.*

Mt. Norquay. At Banff's doorsteps, this small resort has produced many world-class ski racers. It's got plenty of steep runs, and it's intimate and convenient, particularly their economical ski-by-the-hour deals (starting with 2 hr.), meaning you don't have to spend the entire day here to feel like you've gotten your money's worth. This is particularly appealing for beginners and families. On a powder day, head straight to the Memorial Bowl. It's open for night skiing on Fridays 5 to 10pm. *At the end of Mt. Norquay Dr.* ☎ *403/762-4421. www. banffnorquay.com.*

Sunshine Village. Tucked high in the alpine zone in a series of scenic bowls centered around a "village"

Skiing the steep runs at Mt. Norquay.

Sunshine Village ski resort is known for its excellent snow and abundant space.

with a hotel, day lodge, ski school, and gondola station, Sunshine gets fabulous snow and has an abundance of space. It stays open weeks later than the other resorts in Banff, usually until the third week of May. Strawberry and Standish chairs are great for beginners. The Continental Divide has amazing views for intermediate skiers. Goat's Eye Mountain is great for advanced skiers. And only experts need attempt the aptly named Delirium Dive. Advanced snowboarders will find a lot of flat terrain at Sunshine, but the terrain park has grown steadily over the years and is a fun spot for catching some air. *8km (5 miles) west of Banff Townsite at the end of Sunshine Rd.* ☎ *800/661-1676 or 403/762-6500. www.skibanff.com.*

Cross-Country (Nordic) Skiing

A wonderful way to explore the park in winter, cross-country skiing promises great exercise, views, and solitude, if you're seeking it. There are more than 80km (50 miles) of managed trails in Banff National Park, many of them within a half-hour drive of Banff Townsite. The cross-country ski season runs from December to March.

Parks Canada regularly updates trail reports online at www.pc.gc.ca/banff, and ☎ 403/762-1550 for Banff

Ski Big Three

Ski packages that allow you to spend a day at each of Banff's three resorts are offered by the Ski Banff/Lake Louise partnership (P.O. Box 1085, Banff, AB T1L 1H9; ☎ 877/754-7080 or 403/762-4561; www.skibig3.com). Packages include hotel and lift tickets at each of the three resorts. The lift ticket prices for adults range from $265 for 3 out of 4 days to $507 for 6 out of 8 days. It's a great deal and an excellent way to sample Banff's outstanding skiing.

Rent downhill skis and equipment, as well as snowboarding equipment, in Banff at **the Ski Stop** (203A Bear St.; ☎ 403/762-1650) or at the Fairmont Banff Springs Hotel (405 Spray Ave.; ☎ 403/762-5333). In Lake Louise, rent skis, snowshoes, and snowboards at **Wilson Mountain Sports** (p 21). For a ski or snowboard tune-up, try **Ultimate Ski and Ride** (206 Banff Ave.; ☎ 403/762-0547) or **Monod's** (p 87).

Steep & Deep Runs Near Banff

Within a few hours of the Town of Banff, there are two other amazing ski resorts worth a visit, both in the Columbia Valley in British Columbia next door. **Panorama Mountain Resort** (from Hwy. 95, turn west at the Town of Invermere and right onto Panorama Dr., 18km/11 miles to uphill; ☎ 800/663-2929 or 250/342-6941; www.panoramaresort.com) has a whopping 1,220 vertical meters (4,000 vertical ft.) and some deliciously long cruiser runs great for high-level intermediates. There's a cozy village of condos and hotels at the base. At **Kicking Horse Mountain Resort** (from Hwy. 95, turn west at blue sign in downtown Golden, 13km/8 miles uphill; ☎ 866/754-5425 or 250/439-5400; www.kickinghorseresort.com), the snow is famously so light it's called "champagne powder." The resort will appeal mainly to advanced skiers who aren't intimidated by steep terrain and deep snow. Most of the development here has happened since 2002, and the vibe is diehard and earthy.

Townsite area or ☎ 403/522-3833 for Lake Louise.

Rent cross-country equipment at the **Ski Stop** (p 158). In Lake Louise; rent skis and snowshoes at **Wilson Mountain Sports** (p 21).

Beginners The Golf Course Trail has ungroomed trails that are wide open and easy for beginners. There are no defined trails and little elevation gain here, but it's a good place to get a feel for the sport. At Moraine Lake Road, there are 8km (5 miles) of double trackset trails, ideal for a good workout. Flat and wide, trails branch off to the west on the slopes of Mt. Fairview.

Intermediate The Spray River Loop is a 12km (7.8-mile) trail leading behind the Fairmont Banff Springs Hotel with a 200m (656-ft.) elevation gain. Tracks are set for both skate-skiing and classic skiing. It's a good place if you want to go fast. The Pipestone Loops are a wide range of trails across the highway from the Lake Louise village, from 1.9 to 12km (1.2–7.8 miles). All are trackset. Check at the Lake Louise Visitors Centre for updates on trail conditions.

Dog-Sledding

Just over the border from Banff National Park, another classic winter tradition matches tourists up with friendly huskies for a mush across a frozen lake. It's exhilarating. Try **Snowy Owl Sled Dog Tours** (104-602 Bow Valley Trail, Canmore; ☎ 403/678-4369; www.snowyowltours.com). For mushing tours near Lake Louise, contact **Kingmik Dog**

Snowshoeing near Lake Louise.

Banff offers some of the finest ice climbing in the world.

Sled Tours (☎ 403/763-8887; www.kingmikdogsledtours.com).

Ice-Climbing

The frozen waterfalls of Banff National Park offer some of the finest ice climbing in the world. It's an extreme sport that requires proper preparation, but it's also an exhilarating experience—technical, exciting, and beautiful. Learn to climb with the guides at **Yamnuska** (☎ 403/678-4164; www.yamnuska.com).

Ice-Skating

There are a number of places where you can skate outdoors under the winter sky. It's an exhilarating activity that's popular with families. Try the Vermillion Lakes or Johnston

Lake, both just outside the Town of Banff, in the early winter before the snow starts to pile up. There's also a public outdoor rink behind the Fairmont Banff Springs Hotel. At the Fairmont Chateau Lake Louise, there is an outdoor rink on the lake with a spectacular ice castle built right on top. It's a very scenic and romantic place to skate.

Ice Walks

The frozen walls at Johnston Canyon become a winter wonderland, thanks to ice cleats and the guides from **Banff Adventures Unlimited** (211 Bear St.; ☎ 403/762-4554; www.banffadventures.com), who take visitors out for a 4-hour intimate discovery of ice.

Snowshoeing

Strapping on a pair of snowshoes opens up miles and miles of possibilities in Banff, from short strolls near town to big backcountry bowls. Most snowshoe trails follow summer hiking trails—be sure to avoid cross-country trails (groomed or not groomed), as they interfere with the skiing, and be avalanche-aware. Near the townsite, try the flat Fenland Trail. You can also snowshoe at Moose Meadows on the Bow Valley Parkway. More experienced snowshoers will work up a sweat at the Fairview Lookout above Lake Louise. ●

Ice-skating outside the Fairmont Chateau Lake Louise.

Before You Go

Tourist Office

The **Canadian Tourism Commission** (☎ 604/638-8300; www.canada.travel) and **Travel Alberta**, 999 8th St., Calgary (☎ **800/252-3782** or 780/427-4321; www.travelalberta.com) are useful sources of information. The Travel Alberta site is inspiring and helps you understand the breadth of attractions in this province. You can also check out the website for the **Banff Lake Louise Tourism Bureau,** Ste. 375, Cascade Plaza, Banff Avenue (☎ **403/762-8421**; www.banfflakelouise.com).

The Best Time to Go

Summer is the most enjoyable time of the year to be in the Canadian Rockies. However, it's also the most crowded and expensive time. Most hotels double their prices during the high season, which stretches from June through September. So consider the "shoulder seasons." In **June,** the days are luxuriously long and you can catch the early wildflowers in bloom and perhaps even some migrating caribou. In **September,** aspen and larch trees turn golden, but the midday temperature stays gloriously warm.

The Canadian Rockies are also a great destination in winter, by turns cozy, romantic, and peaceful, but also brimming with fun outdoor activities. Banff's star ski resorts—**Sunshine Village, Mount Norquay,** and **Lake Louise**—are among the best in North America. The main businesses in the Town of Banff stay open year-round, with many hotels dropping their prices substantially during the winter season, which runs from **December to**

Previous Page: A welcome sign on the outskirts of Banff.

late March. There are often road closures throughout the Canadian Rockies due to snowfall, especially in the high mountain passes.

Festivals & Special Events

JAN Ice Magic Festival is a stellar ice-carving competition held on the frozen shores of Lake Louise. ☎ *403/762-8421; www.banfflakelouise.com.*

MARCH Lake Louise Loppet is a family-friendly annual cross-country ski race that also attracts Olympians and National Ski Team members. ☎ *403/289-0386; www.calgaryskiclub.org.*

APRIL Join the most radical freestyle skiers and snowboarders at Mount Norquay for the **Spring Fling Big Air Comp and Dummy Downhill.** ☎ *403/762-7703; www.banffnorquay.com.*

MAY The Rocky Mountain Wine & Food Festival is held at the Fairmont Banff Springs Hotel. Sample from the best local bistros and a huge array of wine and spirits from around the world. ☎ *866/228-3555; www.rockymountainwine.com.*

Say farewell to winter with a splash at Sunshine Village's **Slush Cup Beach Party Weekend,** the last weekend of the ski season. Outdoor concerts, a beer garden, and wild folks ski jumping across puddles are highlights. *www.skibanff.com.*

MAY–AUG From drama and opera to jazz and classical music, the **Banff Summer Arts Festival** showcases the best in a variety of artistic areas. If you are an arts lover, don't miss this. ☎ *403/762-6301; www.banffcentre.ca.*

JUNE Teams of 15 runners journey across the Icefields Parkway from

AVERAGE MONTHLY TEMPERATURES & RAINFALL

	JAN	FEB	MAR	APR	MAY	JUNE
High °F/°C	23/–5	32/0	40/4	49/9	57/14	72/20
Low °F/°C	5/–15	13/–11	18/–8	27/–3	31/2	41/5
Days of Precip.	12	10	11	11	16	18

	JULY	AUG	SEPT	OCT	NOV	DEC
High °F/°C	82/25	80/24	66/17	50/10	32/1	23/–5
Low °F/°C	45/7	44/7	38/3	31/–1	18/–8	7/–14
Days of Precip.	19	14	11	11	13	12

Banff to Jasper as part of the annual **Banff to Jasper Relay.** www.bjr.ca.

A recent addition to the local events calendar, **the Banff National Park Bike Fest** brings pedal power to the Rockies for a weekend of road races and fast-paced action. www.banfflakelouise.com.

JULY Held on July 1, **Canada Day** is the anniversary of the signing of the "British North America Act" with the United Kingdom, which created the united country of Canada. Following a free pancake breakfast in Banff's Central Park, pick a good spot on Banff Avenue to take in the parade, with cowboys and marching bands. In the evening, there's live music in the park, and fireworks light up the sky.

AUG Over the first weekend in August, the peaks form an amazing backdrop for 3 days of music at the annual **Canmore Folk Music Festival,** Alberta's longest-running folk music festival. ☎ 403/678-2524, www.canmorefolkfestival.com.

Since 1926, Jasper has hosted the **Jasper Heritage Pro Rodeo,** featuring bareback, saddle bronc, steer wrestling, and barrel racing. There's a Western dance, barbecue, and kids' rodeo held in town. ☎ 780/852-4622; www.jasperheritagerodeo.com.

Banff's many heritage buildings welcome visitors during **Doors Open Banff** for self-guided heritage tours. ☎ 403/762-8421; www.doorsopenalberta.ca.

SEPT A Banff tradition that draws runners from across Western Canada, **Melissa's Road Race** has a 10K (6.2 mile) and 22K (13.7 mile) road route, with proceeds going to the Banff community. It sells out months ahead of time, but spectators can catch the action at the finish line at the Banff Recreational Grounds. www.melissasroadrace.ca.

OCT–NOV Each year, the Banff Centre hosts the **Banff Mountain Film and Book Festivals** celebrating the spirit of those who live in the mountains. If you're a keen armchair adventurer, it's best to buy a weekend pass, which will get you into plenty of screenings as well as to hear guest speakers and rub shoulders with some of the finest adventurers from around the world. ☎ 403/762-6301; www.banffcentre.ca.

DEC From a World Cup ski race to a Santa Claus Parade, winter gets a kick-start during the annual **Winter-Start Festival.** ☎ 403/762-8421; www.banfflakelouise.com.

The Weather

Despite the Canadian Rockies' northerly latitude, the climate actually resembles that of the Rocky Mountains south of the United States border because the altitude isn't as high as it is in the U.S. Rockies. Snow at lower elevations usually disappears by May, but sometimes hangs around the higher elevations well into the summer. Although it often rains for at least a week in June, and you can expect a cold rain or wet snowfall in July, the summer climate is generally very pleasant, with warm days and low humidity. Evenings almost always require a sweater. Rain clouds often gather along the Continental Divide, so don't be disappointed to come all the way here and not be able to see the high peaks right away. July temperatures typically hit 68° to 77°F (20°–25°C). Spring and fall days are usually fine and bright, though evenings can be cool.

In January, though the lows can drop way down to −22°F (−30°C), the winter sunshine and blue skies are the stuff of legend.

Useful Websites

In addition to the websites at the opening of this chapter, check out:

- **www.parkscanada.gc.ca**: Incredibly useful information on all of the area's national parks.

- **www.mountainnature.com**: Great information on the natural history of the area.

- **www.icefieldsparkway.ca**: A new, interactive website that offers a virtual tour of one of the world's most beautiful drives.

- **www.banff.com**: A site with events listings, virtual tours, weather updates, and listings for everything from restaurants to ski-rental shops.

- **www.banff.ca**: The site for the Town of Banff has useful information for visitors, including information on the public-transit system.

Cellphones

The cellular phone coverage in the Canadian Rockies is spotty. In the Town of Banff, as in other towns like Canmore, Lake Louise, and Jasper, coverage is good. In between these spots, though, it is not reliable. For example, your coverage will likely cut out as you drive from Banff to Lake Louise. Phones using CDMA network technology—currently the most common type in use in both Canada and the U.S.—will work in Canada in places with reception. GSM/GPRS phones—the dominant standard pretty much everywhere else—also work here, thanks to roaming agreements. Before leaving home, be sure to update your phone's roaming software to assure good connectivity. And check with your provider to see what kind of international usage fees may apply. For information on land lines and international calls, see "Telephones" in "Fast Facts," later.

Car Rentals

Most visitors to Banff and Jasper national parks will fly to either Calgary or Edmonton and rent a car to get to the parks. Though shuttle service is available from the Calgary International Airport to several locations around Banff (see "By Plane" below), it's a good idea to rent a car to get around for the duration of your trip.

Getting **There**

By Plane

Both the **Calgary International Airport** (☎ 877/254-7427 or

403/735-1200; www.calgaryairport. com) and the **Edmonton International Airport** (☎ 800/268-7134;

www.edmontonairports.com) service the Canadian Rockies. If you are heading to Banff National Park, fly to Calgary and from there take the **Banff Airporter** (☎ 888/449-2901 or 403/762-3330; www.banffair porter.com; $58 one-way or $115 round-trip). Banff is 129km/80 miles west of Calgary. It's about 90 minutes by car from the airport. If you want to visit Jasper National Park first, fly to Edmonton (363km/225 miles east of Jasper; a 4-hr. trip by car). Many people visiting Jasper go first to Banff via Calgary and then drive north. Others do the trip in reverse.

By Car

If you're driving into Banff National Park from the east, take the **Trans-Canada Highway (Hwy. 1)** west from Calgary. The park's eastern gate is 129km (80 miles) west of the **Calgary International Airport,** just west of the town of Canmore. If you are coming to Banff from the west, you have two options. From central British Columbia, you can take the Trans-Canada Highway east via the town of **Golden, BC,** and Yoho National Park, and enter Banff just west of the village of Lake Louise.

The other option, from southeastern British Columbia, is to take Hwy. 93 north into Banff via the town of **Radium Hot Springs, BC,** and Kootenay National Park. See chapter 5 for more information on planning a side trip to Golden, BC, or Radium Hot Springs, BC.

If you're approaching the parks from the city of Edmonton, which is to the north, you'll get to Jasper National Park first. Take **Hwy. 16** (the Yellowhead Hwy.) west to Jasper National Park's eastern gate (363km/225 miles west of Edmonton International Airport). From north-central British Columbia, you can take Hwy. 16 east to Jasper National Park via **Prince George, BC,** and Mount Robson Provincial Park.

Vancouver is 858km (532 miles) west of Banff and 863km (535 miles) west of Jasper.

By Train

VIA Rail Canada (☎ 888/842-7245; www.viarail.ca) services Jasper National Park on its Edmonton–Vancouver run, which takes about 16 hours direct. Most trains from major Canadian and U.S. centers connect to this route. Check with VIA Rail Canada or with **Amtrak** (☎ 800/872-7245; www.amtrak.com).

There is no VIA Rail Canada service to Banff or Calgary; however, **Rocky Mountaineer Railtours** (☎ 877/460-3200; www.rocky mountaineer.com) has a stunning overnight trip that departs from Vancouver and stops in either Banff or Jasper (you select your destination at the changeover in Kamloops, BC). **Royal Canadian Pacific Luxury Rail Tours** (☎ 877/665-3044; www.royalcanadianpacific.com) has a 6-day tour on a luxury heritage rail car that leaves Calgary, passes through the Canadian Rockies south of Banff, and loops back through Golden and Banff to Calgary.

By Bus

Greyhound Bus Lines (☎ 800/661-8747; www.greyhound.ca) has multiple arrivals daily through Banff and Jasper going both east and west. Their routes from Vancouver to Calgary stop in Canmore, Banff, Field, and Golden. **Brewster** (☎ 877/791-5500; www.brewster.ca) has daily trips from Vancouver to Edmonton and Jasper, including a 2-day drive that includes an overnight stop midway.

Getting **Around**

By Shuttle

There are a number of shuttle services to help ease your travel between Banff and Jasper national parks. **Sundog Tours** (☎ 888/786-3641 or 780/852-4056; www.sundogtours.com) runs between Banff, Lake Louise, and Jasper daily (except on poor winter-driving days and from Nov through late Dec). Some daily departures hit all the major attractions along the way; others go directly from Jasper to Lake Louise or Banff. The Jasper–Banff trip costs $69 per adult and $39 per child 12 and under; the Jasper–Lake Louise trip costs $59 per adult and $35 per child. **Brewster's Explore Rockies** (☎ 877/791-5500 or 403/762-6700; www.brewster.ca), the original tour company in Banff and Jasper, has a slew of shuttle services and day tours between Banff, Jasper, Calgary, and Edmonton, including a 9½-hour day trip that starts in Banff and ends in the Town of Jasper. It costs $115 for adults and $60 for children ages 5 to 15. Children 4 and under ride free. The tour does not include their Columbia Icefield excursion.

By Car

If you are staying in the Town of Banff and not really planning on trips outside of it, you can take a shuttle from the Calgary airport and then walk, take the local ROAM public bus system, or a short cab ride to most attractions in town. However, if you plan on seeing any of the rest of the park, including Lake Louise, as well as making a trip to Jasper, then having your own vehicle is a major advantage. It can be hard to get to trail heads, although ski resorts run shuttles during the winter.

There is little to no public transport between main destinations in the Canadian Rockies, and taxi services are very expensive—not to mention restricting, since your movements are governed by their schedule. The roads are in good condition most of the year (you don't really need to rent an expensive four-wheel-drive sport-utility vehicle except during major snowstorms), and driving here is a relaxing way to soak up the gorgeous scenery.

The one down side of renting a car is that parking can be a problem in the Town of Banff and at Lake Louise. Stick to the big parking lots (in Banff there is a covered multistory parkade on Bear St. btw. Caribou and Buffalo sts.; in Lake Louise at the Samson Mall; and in Jasper beside the Heritage Railway Station). For more information, see chapter 4.

By RV

They're not for everyone, but most people who try it discover what a joy it is to travel by recreational vehicle. It affords a level of independence and comfort that car travel can't. And finding a quiet campground by a river is as close to the camping experience as you can get without giving up your pillow and mattress.

More than half of the campgrounds in Banff and Jasper national parks accommodate RVs, trailers, and camper vans, and you must stay in these designated areas. In addition to navigating around campgrounds, RV drivers need to know how to get around town, too. In the Town of Banff, there is a trailer drop-off site in the industrial area at the northeast end of Banff Avenue.

You can leave your trailer here and take the car or RV itself through the streets of town. There are also a number of larger parking lots that accommodate RVs, including one near the Mineral Springs Hospital on Gopher Street and another one across from the post office on Buffalo Street, along the Bow River.

Many people come to the Rockies in an RV they've rented at the airport in Edmonton or Calgary.

For RV rentals, contact **Cana-Dream** (2510 27th St. NE, Calgary, AB T1Y 7G1; ☎ 800/461-7368 or 403/291-1000; www.canadream. com).

Fast **Facts**

ATMS   Banff does have its share of Automated Teller Machines, which operate on the worldwide **Cirrus** (☎ 800/424-7787; www.master card.com), **PLUS** (☎ 800/843-7587; www.visa.com), and **Interac** (☎ 416/362-8550; www.interac.ca) networks. Be sure you know your personal identification number (PIN) before you leave home, and be sure your daily withdrawal limit will cover the amount of cash you'll need. Note that ATM fees can be higher for international transactions than for domestic. **Alberta Treasury's** branch is at 317 Banff Ave. (☎ 403/762-8505). In Lake Louise there is an ATM in Samson Mall (☎ 403/522-3678). The **Bank of Montreal** is at 107 Banff Ave. (☎ 403/762-2275), and the **Canadian Imperial Bank of Canada** (CIBC) is at 98 Banff Ave. (☎ 403/762-3317).

BANKING HOURS   Banks are generally open Mon–Fri 9:30am–4:30pm, though some branches have hours on weekends as well.

BIKE RENTALS   Bike shops will likely try to rent you their most expensive bikes. If you're a beginner mountain biker, however, and will only be heading out on a few trails around town, you do not need a full-suspension bike. If you want to just cruise the main, paved, trails of the townsite, go for an inexpensive bike.

You can rent both road and mountain bikes in Banff National Park at **BacTrax Bike Rentals** (225 Bear St.; ☎ 403/762-8177). Guided tours of the Vermillion Lakes and Sundance Canyon leave daily. In addition to renting regular-size bikes for adult riders, **Adventures Unlimited** (211 Bear St.; ☎ 403/762-4554) rents kids' bikes, trailers, and strollers, too. In Lake Louise, rent bikes at **Wilson Mountain Sports** (Samson Mall; ☎ 403/522-3636). In Jasper, the folks at **Freewheel Cycle** (681 Patricia St.; ☎ 780/852-3898; www.freewheel jasper.com) are the local experts on two-wheeling. They rent front-suspension mountain bikes that can also be used on roads. You can rent both road and mountain bikes from **Jasper Source for Sports** (406 Patricia St.; ☎ 780/852-3654).

BUSINESS HOURS   Hours vary by shop, but as a general rule most open daily around 10am and stay open until at least 6pm. Shops in the Town of Banff usually stay open later. Most are open daily, though some close on Sunday.

CONSULATES & EMBASSIES   The **U.S. Consulate** is at Ste. 1000, 615 Macleod Trail SW, Calgary (☎ 403/266-8962). The **British Consulate** is at Ste. 3000, 150 6th Ave. SW, Calgary (☎ 403/705-1755). The **Irish Consulate** is at

3803 8th A St. SW, Calgary (☎ 403/243-2970). The nearest **Australian Consulate** is at 2050 1075 W. Georgia St., Vancouver (☎ 604/694-6160). The consulate of **New Zealand** is at 888 Dunsmuir St., Ste. 1200, Vancouver (☎ 604/684-7388).

CURRENCY EXCHANGE Currency exchange counters can be found at the airport, but you'll get a better rate just using ATMs (p 167) or at the **Custom House Global Foreign Exchange,** at 211 Banff Ave. (☎ 403/760-6630).

In Jasper, there is a currency exchange house in **Whistlers Inn** (105 Miette Ave.; ☎ 780/852-3361). Be sure to check current exchange rates before your trip via www.xe.com or any of the other major currency trackers.

CUSTOMS Non-Canadian residents will pass through **Canada Border Services** (☎ 800/461-9999 or 204/983-3500; www.cbsa-asfc.gc.ca) upon arriving in the country. If you're concerned about items you intend to bring into the country, check the website's "Information for Visitors" section. U.S. citizens will pass through **U.S. Customs** (☎ 877/CBP-5511 [227-5511]; www.cbp.gov) on departure from Canada. The standard personal duty-free allowance for U.S. citizens returning from Canada is US$800. There are also limits on the amount of alcoholic beverages (usually 1L), cigarettes (1 carton), cigars (100 total, and no Cubans), and other tobacco products you may include in your personal duty-free exemption. **Joint Customs declarations** are possible for family members traveling together. For instance, for a husband and wife with two children, the total duty-free exemption would be US$3,200. Note that most meat or meat products, fruits, plants, vegetables, or plant-derived

products will be seized by U.S. Customs agents unless they're accompanied by an import license from a U.S. government agency.

For more specifics, visit the **U.S. Customs Service** website (www.cbp.gov). U.K. citizens should visit the **U.K. Customs and Excise** site (www.hmce.gov.uk); Australians should go to the **Australia Customs Service** (www.customs.gov.au); Kiwis should check the **New Zealand Customs Service** (www.customs.govt.nz); and citizens of Ireland should check the **Irish Revenue** site (www.revenue.ie).

DENTISTS Most major hotels have a dentist on call. **Banff Dental Care** is at 220 Bear St. (☎ 403/762-3979). Call first for an appointment. The clinic is open Monday and Wednesday 8am to 5pm, Tuesday and Thursday 9am to 6pm, and Friday 8am to 1pm.

DINING Eating out will be one of your highlights in Banff. For the most popular spots, reservations are recommended and are essential on Saturday evenings or long weekends.

DOCTORS Hotels usually have a doctor on call. **Alpine Medical Clinic,** 201A-211 Bear St. (☎ 403/762-3155), is a drop-in clinic open Monday through Thursday 8:30am to 7pm, Friday 8am to 5pm, and weekends 9am to 5pm.

ELECTRICITY Outlets and voltage (110 volts AC) are the same in Canada as in the United States, so laptops, chargers, hair dryers, and other small appliances from the U.S. will work just fine. Appliances from some other countries that work on a different voltage will require an adapter and/or converter.

EMBASSIES See "Consulates & Embassies" above.

EMERGENCIES For emergencies in the Canadian Rockies, dial ☎ 911.

EVENT LISTINGS Event listings are posted online by the **Banff–Lake Louise Tourism Bureau** at www. banfflakelouise.com. The free local weekly newspaper **Rocky Mountain Outlook** (www.rmoutlook.ca) also is a great source for updated arts, sports, and community events. It's published on Thursdays and available throughout Banff.

FAMILY TRAVEL Banff and the Canadian Rockies are fantastically kid-friendly. Family travel websites include **Family Travel Forum** (www.familytravelforum.com), a comprehensive site that offers customized trip planning; **Family Travel Network** (www.familytravel network.com), an online magazine providing travel tips; and **Travel-withyourkids.com** (www.travel withyourkids.com), a comprehensive site written by parents for parents offering sound advice for long-distance and international travel with children.

GAY & LESBIAN TRAVELERS Mountain Pride (☎ 800/958-9621; www. gaybanff.com) is a social networking group for Banff residents and visitors. **Banff Gay Weddings** (☎ 403/609-3896; www.banffgayweddings. com) organizes same-sex ceremonies and events. While Alberta is perhaps the most conservative province in Canada, Banff and its neighboring towns are gay-friendly.

HOLIDAYS Alberta has 12 public holidays throughout the year, when banks, government offices, schools, and some shops are closed: New Year's Day (Jan 1), Family Day (third Mon in Feb), Good Friday (the Fri before Easter), Easter Monday (the day after), Victoria Day (the Mon before May 25), Canada Day (July 1), Heritage Day (first Mon in Aug), Labour Day (first Mon in Sept), Thanksgiving (second Mon in Oct), Remembrance Day (Nov 11), Christmas (Dec 25), and Boxing Day (Dec 26).

INSURANCE The cost of travel insurance varies widely, depending on the destination, the cost and length of your trip, your age and health, and the type of trip you're taking. You can get estimates from various providers through **InsureMyTrip. com** (www.insuremytrip.com). Enter your trip cost and dates, your age, and other information, for prices from more than a dozen companies.

Medical Insurance: Most U.S. health plans do not provide coverage outside of the U.S., and the ones that do often require you to pay for services upfront and reimburse you only after you return home. As a safety net, you may want to buy travel medical insurance from providers like **MEDEX Assistance** (☎ 410/453-6300; www.medexassist.com) or **Travel Assistance International** (☎ 800/821-2828; www.travel assistance.com).

Trip-Cancellation Insurance: Trip-cancellation insurance typically covers you if you have to back out of a trip (due to illness and so on), if your travel supplier goes bankrupt, if there's a natural disaster, or if your government advises against travel to your destination. Some plans cover cancellations for any reason. **TravelSafe** (☎ 888/885-7233; www.travelsafe.com) offers both types of coverage. **Expedia** (www. expedia.com) also offers any-reason cancellation coverage for its air-hotel packages. Other recommended insurers include: **Access America** (☎ 866/807-3982; www. accessamerica.com); **Travel Guard International** (☎ 800/826-4919; www.travelguard.com); **Travel Insured International** (☎ 800/243-3174; www.travelinsured.com); and **Travelex Insurance Services** (☎ 888/457-4602; www.travelex-insurance.com).

Lost-Luggage Insurance: If your luggage is lost, immediately file a lost-luggage claim at the airport, detailing the luggage contents. Most airlines require that you report delayed, damaged, or lost baggage within 4 hours of arrival. On international flights, baggage coverage is limited to approximately US$9.07 per pound, up to approximately US$635 per checked bag. If you plan to check items more valuable than what's covered by the standard liability, see if your homeowner's policy covers your valuables, or get baggage insurance as part of your comprehensive travel-insurance package.

INTERNET ACCESS Almost all hotels in the Canadian Rockies now provide some kind of Internet access, either wireless, wired, or via a business center. There are also free Wi-Fi hot spots in many locations around town, often in coffee shops.

LIQUOR LAWS The legal drinking age in Alberta is 18. In British Columbia it is 19. Bars, lounges, and restaurants that serve alcohol all close between midnight and 2am, depending on when they got their liquor license. Hard liquor, beer, and wine are available at privately owned liquor stores in Alberta. Specialty wine stores (p 86 lists some of the best) mostly stick to the grape, but usually also carry a small selection of beer and spirits.

LOST PROPERTY Lost items are often turned in to the **Town of Banff,** where they are kept for 30 days. Contact ☎ **403-762-1218** daily between 8am and 6pm for inquiries. There is also an online Lost Property Report available at the town's website, www.banff.ca. Outside the Town of Banff, try **Parks Canada** at ☎ **403-762-1550.**

If you lose your passport, contact your country's embassy or consulate immediately (see "Consulates & Embassies," above).

MAIL & POSTAGE Mailing a letter within Canada costs 61¢. To the U.S., it's $1.05. To all other international destinations, it's $1.80. The main **post office** in Banff is at 204 Buffalo St. (☎ **403-762-2586;** www.canadapost.ca), across from Central Park. You can also buy stamps at many drugstores and convenience stores.

MONEY Canada's money is denominated the same as U.S. dollars, except its C$1 and C$2 denominations are coins rather than bills. The C$1 coin is known as a "loonie" as it has the image of a common loon on one side. The C$2 coin is known as a "toonie," for obvious comedic reasons. For more info, see "Currency Exchange," p 168.

NEWSPAPERS & MAGAZINES The major newspapers in Alberta are the *Calgary Herald* (www.calgary herald.com) and the *Edmonton Journal* (www.theprovince.com), which both publish 7 days a week.

The local weekly newspapers in Banff are the **Rocky Mountain Outlook** (www.rmoutlook.com), which publishes every Thursday, and the **Banff Crag and Canyon** (www.banffcragandcanyon.com), which hits stands on Tuesdays.

PARKING See "Getting Around: By Car," p 166.

PASSPORTS U.S. citizens traveling to Canada by any means— air, sea, car, bus, train, or on foot— will need a passport but no visa. The same applies for citizens of the United Kingdom, Australia, Ireland, and New Zealand. If you're a citizen of another country, check the **Canada Border Services Agency** website, www.cbsa-asfc.gc.ca/travel-voyage, for specific requirements.

For safety, make two photocopies of your passport before leaving home. Take one set with you as a backup (keeping it separate from the original) and leave one at home.

PERMITS Every visitor to a national park is required to have a permit (also known as a pass). You can pick one up at a park gate or information center inside the park. Permits are valid in all Canadian Rocky Mountain national parks (Banff, Jasper, Yoho, Kootenay, Waterton Lakes, and Glacier national parks). A day pass costs $9.80 for adults, $8.30 for seniors, and $4.90 for children. More economical is the Annual Pass, which is a good idea if you're planning to stay for a few days and visit more than one park. It's valid for 1 year from the purchase date for unlimited entries to every one of Canada's national parks, coast to coast. Individual rates are $68 for adults, $58 for seniors, and $33 for children ages 6 to 12. The pass is free for children ages 5 and under. For groups of 2 to 7, this pass costs $136, making it the best deal for most visitors. Rates are expected to rise in 2013.

Permits are also required for backcountry camping and fishing inside the National Parks. For more information, visit www.pc.gc.ca.

PET-FRIENDLY TRAVEL While there are a few hotels in Banff that welcome pets, in general the Canadian Rockies aren't particularly pet-friendly. This is mainly due to the importance placed on the health of the local wildlife populations. Keep your dog on a leash at all times, especially in campgrounds and on hiking trails. To wildlife like elk, wolves, bears, and cougars, your dog may look an awful lot like dinner. Avoid any areas in the parks where the potential for wildlife encounters is high (ask at an information center), and take your dog for a walk only during daylight hours. Do not leave your dog unattended outside. Unrestrained pets have been known to harass wildlife, provoke attacks, and endanger people. And please pick up after your pooch—the "leave no trace" principle applies to pets, too.

PHARMACIES The biggest pharmacy in the Town of Banff is **Rexall Drug Store,** lower level of Cascade Plaza, 317 Banff Ave. (☎ **403/762-2245**).

POLICE Call ☎ **911** for emergencies.

SAFETY Don't drink the water from any streams, rivers, or lakes in Banff or Jasper national parks. A waterborne parasite called *Giardia lamblia* can cause an illness known in Canada as "beaver fever." It is transmitted via infected animal feces and can cause serious and prolonged gastrointestinal problems.

Also be on the lookout for **wood ticks**—small, flat-bodied, spider-like insects that bite humans and can carry **Rocky Mountain spotted fever** and **Lyme disease** (although the latter is rare in the northern Rockies). They usually abound in dry, grassy slopes in the spring. If you're hiking through such an area, give yourself a good once-over at the end of the day. If in doubt, drop by the **Mineral Springs Hospital** in Banff to see a doctor (301 Lynx St.; ☎ **403/762-2222**). In Jasper, go to **Seton General Hospital** (518 Robson St.; ☎ **780/852-3344**). There has been no evidence of West Nile virus in the Canadian Rockies.

Hiking in the mountains is so beautiful that it may make you feel lightheaded. But lightheadedness may also be a sign of **altitude sickness.** Although elevations in the Canadian Rockies aren't as high as in the Colorado and Montana Rockies, you can still feel the altitude. People with severe heart or lung conditions should take note. Others should bring along some headache medicine and drink plenty of water.

You'll also be closer to the sun in the mountains, so wear a **sun hat** and **sunscreen.** Beyond the sun, cold and rain are the other weather factors that could hamper your holiday. Check the latest weather forecast before heading out. Always pack a rain jacket and warm clothing in your daypack. And always carry a **first-aid kit,** both in your car and in your pack. At the very least, it should include latex gloves (to prevent spreading infections), butterfly bandages, sterile gauze pads, adhesive tape, antibiotic ointment, pain relievers (for kids and adults), alcohol pads, knife, scissors, and tweezers.

Hiking in Banff involves moving through bear country and you should be prepared to encounter a bear at any time. Carry bear spray and know how to use it. Make noise while you hike, keep your dog on a leash, and hike in groups. Pick up the "Hiking in Bear Country" pamphlet from Parks Canada for more information.

In terms of personal safety in the mountains, be aware that almost any slope is a potential **avalanche** chute—and even small avalanches can be deadly. Drivers should avoid stopping in places where there are signs that read NO STOPPING, AVALANCHE AREA, and anyone venturing into the backcountry—especially in winter—should know how to recognize and travel in avalanche terrain. Call ☎ **403/762-1460** in Banff or ☎ **780/852-6176** in Jasper for the latest avalanche hazard reports from Parks Canada.

There is also a risk of getting hit by falling rock and ice or slipping into a glacier crevasse, particularly in Jasper National Park. Do not ignore the signs telling you to stay back from the **Angel Glacier** at **Mt. Edith Cavell** or the **Athabasca Glacier,** both in Jasper. These can be—and have been—deadly.

Don't leave valuables in your car or unattended in public places. This also applies to hiking trail heads.

The Canadian Government website (**www.safecanada.ca**) has a list of safety tips in case you need something to worry about.

SENIOR TRAVELERS Shops, hotels, attractions, and services throughout Western Canada often offer discounts for people 65 and over.

SMOKING Smoking is prohibited in all public places in Alberta and British Columbia, including bars, clubs, and restaurants.

TAXES All hotels, restaurants, gift shops, and services charge the 5% goods and services tax (GST) on all purchases. (**Note:** A program that allowed foreigners to receive a rebate for the GST spent during their time in Canada was canceled in 2007.) There is no provincial sales tax in Alberta. In British Columbia, a provincial sales tax of 7% is charged on purchased goods.

TELEPHONES Dialing within Alberta requires you to use full 10-digit phone numbers, including the area code, of which there are two in Alberta: 403 and 780. To reach the British Columbia side of the Canadian Rockies, first dial 250. **Phoning between the U.S. and Canada** requires no special trick: Just dial 1 plus the area code and local number, as you would between states in the U.S. **To dial other countries** direct from Banff, dial the international access code (011), followed by the relevant country code (61 for Australia, 353 for Ireland, 64 for New Zealand, and 44 for the U.K.) and the local number with area code, if applicable. **To call Banff from outside North America,** dial the international access code (00 from the U.K., Ireland, or New Zealand, or 0011 from Australia), the country code (1), and then the local number with area code. For information on cellphone service, see "Cellphones," p 164.

TIME ZONE Alberta and the B.C. Rockies are located in the Mountain time zone, 7 hours behind Greenwich Mean Time (changing to the Pacific time zone between Golden and Revelstoke). The area observes daylight saving time from the second Sunday in March to the first Sunday in November.

TIPPING Customary tipping amounts are the same in Banff and the rest of Canada as in major U.S. cities, with a target of 15% for restaurants and taxis. (Though many people round that up to 20%.) If porters help with you bags at hotels or airports, the usual tip is $1 per bag (or $2 if it's heavy).

TOILETS Public toilets are increasingly easy to find in Banff. In fact, there are now nine facilities dotted around the main area of town, including the Whyte Museum, the Public Library, and Cascade Plaza. You can also find facilities at the corner of Wolf Street and Banff Avenue, and in the Parks Canada Administration Building, just across the Bow River Bridge. In Lake Louise, there are facilities in the Visitor Centre, in the main parking lot at the lakeshore, and in the Fairmont Chateau Lake Louise.

TOURIST OFFICES The following on-the-ground tourist centers can help with information, maps, suggestions, and booking accommodations: **Banff Information Centre** is at 224 Banff Ave. (☎ **403/762-1550**), and there is a similar location at the **Lake Louise Visitor Centre**, in Samson Mall, 101 Lake Louise Dr. (☎ **403/522-3833**). **Jasper National Park's Information Centre** is at 500 Connaught Dr. (☎ **780/852-6716**). Just before you enter Banff National Park, you can visit the **Travel Alberta Visitor Information Centre** in Canmore at 2801 Bow Valley Trail (☎ **800/252-3782** or 403/678-5277), which is right off the Trans-Canada Hwy. 1.

TOURS **Brewster** (P.O. Box 1140, Banff, AB T1L 1J3; ☎ **877/791-5500** or 403/762-6700; www.brewster.ca) knows Banff better than any other tour operator and has a long history of guiding here to prove it. It offers many sightseeing tours in both Banff and Jasper. Taking even the 3-hour **Discover Banff with Banff Gondola tour** will teach you more than you'll ever learn on your own. If you're going to British Columbia, sign up for Brewster's **Rockies Discovery** 3-day, 2-night tour that stops in Calgary, Banff, Lake Louise, Roger's Pass, and Kamloops.

Discover Banff Tours (215 Banff Ave., P.O. Box 1566, Banff, AB T1L 1B5; ☎ **877/565-9372** or 403/760-5007; www.banfftours.com) leads small groups on interpretive tours of all the highlights in Banff National Park, including the Town of Banff, Lake Louise, and Moraine Lake, as well as the Icefields Parkway. Morning and evening wildlife-viewing tours are really nice.

TRAVELERS WITH DISABILITIES The museums and visitor centers in Banff are all wheelchair-accessible. Most hotels now have at least one wheelchair-accessible room. The **Upper Hot Springs** in Banff National Park and the Radium Hot Springs in Kootenay National Park are friendly to those with mobility restraints.

If you are planning on car camping, head for **Tunnel Mountain, Johnston Canyon, Lake Louise,** or **Waterfowl Lakes campgrounds.** In Jasper National Park, try **Whistlers, Wapiti, or Wabasso.**

Signs clearly mark which trails in the parks are paved. In Banff, try the asphalt-covered **Sundance Trail.** There is an adjustable-height viewing scope at **Bow Summit.** The Lakeside Trail at **Lake Louise** is another wheelchair-accessible trail.

Wheelchair-friendly trails in Jasper include the **Clifford E. Lee Trail** at Lake Edith/Annette and the **Maligne Lake Trail,** as well as points along **Maligne Canyon,** at **Pyramid Island,** and the interpretive loop at the **Pocahontas Coal Mine Trail.**

WEIGHTS & MEASURES Canada uses the metric system. Remember: 1km=0.62 miles, 1 liter=0.26 gallons, 1 kilogram=2.2 pounds, and Celsius temperatures are based on 0 being the freezing point (in Fahrenheit measurement it's 32).

A Brief **History**

175 MILLION YEARS AGO The Rocky Mountains are formed as the Pacific tectonic plate moves under the North American plate.

11,000 B.C. Early archaeological records date the presence of peoples like the Crees, Kootenays, and Plains Blackfoot to have lived, fished, and hunted in the vast Rocky Mountains.

1754 The first recorded visit of a European to the Rockies is made by Anthony Hendy.

1800 Legendary explorer and map-maker David Thompson explores the Bow Valley.

1841 George Simpson, the Governor of the Hudson's Bay Company, is the first known European to visit the Town of Banff area.

1871 As part of a deal to unite British Columbia with the rest of Canada, the Canadian government forms the Canadian Pacific Railway (CPR) to construct a railway across the new nation.

1882 Tom Wilson, a CPR guide, becomes the first non-Native man to see Lake Louise, with the help of his Stoney partner.

1883 Three railway workers stumble upon a series of hot springs on the lower slopes of Sulphur Mountain.

1885 Canada's first national park is formed in Banff, preserving 26 sq. km (10 sq. miles) surrounding the hot springs. The reserve is increased to 670 sq. km (259 sq. miles) in 1887, and 7,125 sq. km (2,751 sq. miles) in 1917.

1886 Construction of the Canadian Pacific Railway is completed. Banff is named after the Scottish district "Banffshire," birthplace of two of the CPR's directors, Lord Strathcona and George Stephen.

1888 The CPR opens the elegant log-framed 250-room Banff Springs Hotel, the most expensive hotel in the world at the time.

1890 A log cabin is built on the shores of Lake Louise, soon to be replaced by a larger "chateau."

1917 The Federal Government passes the first National Parks Act in the world.

1921 A road is completed linking Banff and Lake Louise, ushering in the era of car-based tourism.

1928 A log cabin is built at the site of today's Sunshine Village as a stopover for horse trekkers.

1936 Temple Lodge is built across the Bow Valley from Lake Louise, the beginning of the Lake Louise ski resort's history.

1941   The first rope tows are installed at Sunshine Village ski resort.

1956   The Trans-Canada Hwy. 1 is completed through Banff and Yoho national parks.

1961   Paving of the Icefields Parkway is completed.

1985   Banff, Jasper, Yoho, and Kootenay national parks, along with four adjacent provincial parks, are declared a World Heritage Site by the United Nations Educational, Scientific and Cultural Organization (UNESCO).

1990   Thanks to a joint agreement between local citizens and the federal and provincial

governments, Banff becomes a self-governing municipality within the Province of Alberta, the only incorporated municipality within a Canadian national park.

1998   The Delirium Dive area, a mecca for extreme skiers, is re-opened at Sunshine Village.

1999   Parks Canada begins requiring hikers to travel in tight groups of four in high grizzly bear territory, especially around Moraine Lake during peak summer hiking season.

2007   Banff's downtown core undergoes a redevelopment to replace dated infrastructure, making it more pedestrian friendly.

Airline Websites

AIR CANADA
www.aircanada.ca
ALASKA AIRLINES
www.alaskaair.com
AMERICAN AIRLINES
www.aa.com
BRITISH AIRWAYS
www.british-airways.com
DELTA AIR LINES
www.delta.com

FRONTIER AIRLINES
www.frontierairlines.com
UNITED AIRLINES
www.united.com
US AIRWAYS
www.usairways.com
WESTJET
www.westjet.com

Index

See also Accommodations and Restaurant indexes, below.

Photo **Credits**

p. i: © Gary Pearl / StockShot / Alamy Images; p. i: © Imagebroker / Thomas Sbampato Alamy Images; p. i: © George Ostertag / SuperStock / Alamy Images; p. ii, top: © Claire Dibble; p. ii, second: © Andrew Hempstead; p. ii, middle: Courtesy Fairmont Hotels & Resorts; p. ii, fourth: © Sue G. PR / Frommers.com Community; p. ii, bottom: © John E Marriott / All Canada Photos / SuperStock; p. iii, top: © Claire Dibble; p. iii, second: © Claire Dibble; p. iii, middle: © Andrew Hempstead; p. iii, fourth: © Claire Dibble; p. iii, bottom: © Photo by Richard Halman, Courtesy Sunshine Village; p. 1: © Claire Dibble; p. 3: © Andrew Hempstead; p. 4, top: © Andrew Hempstead; p. 4, bottom: © Serge Desrosiers / Frommers.com Community; p. 5: © Andrew Hempstead; p. 6: © CCinCalif / Frommers.com Community; p. 7: © Andrew Hempstead; p. 9: © Andrew Hempstead; p. 10, top: © Claire Dibble; p. 10, bottom: © Andrew Hempstead; p. 11: Courtesy Fairmont Hotels & Resorts; p. 13, top: © Andrew Hempstead; p. 13, bottom: © Andrew Hempstead; p. 14: Courtesy Fairmont Hotels & Resorts; p. 15: © mlorenz / Frommers.com Community; p. 16: © bonners1980@yahoo.com / Frommers.com Community; p. 17, top: © Claire Dibble; p. 17, bottom: © elleonora / Frommers.com Community; p. 19: © Andrew Hempstead; p. 20, top: © Claire Dibble; p. 20, bottom: © Brian Leroy / Frommers.com Community; p. 21: © Linda Plummer / Frommers.com Community; p. 23: © kmaltagliati / Frommers.com Community; p. 24: © Claire Dibble; p. 25, top: © Claire Dibble; p. 25, bottom: © Andrew Hempstead; p. 26, top: © Claire Dibble; p. 26, bottom: © Claire Dibble; p. 28: © Claire Dibble; p. 29: © Andrew Hempstead; p. 30: Courtesy Fairmont Hotels & Resorts; p. 31: © Sue G. PR / Frommers.com Community; p. 33: © Tando / Frommers.com Community; p. 34: © Andrew Hempstead; p. 35: © Matthewas / Frommers.com Community; p. 37: © Andrew Hempstead; p. 38, top: © Andrew Hempstead; p. 38, bottom: © Andrew Hempstead; p. 39: Courtesy of Fairmont Hotels & Resorts; p. 41: © Andrew Hempstead; p. 42, top: © Andrew Hempstead; p. 42, bottom: Courtesy of Fairmont Hotels & Resorts; p. 43: © Photo by Richard Halman, Courtesy Sunshine Village; p. 45: © Claire Dibble; p. 46, top: © Claire Dibble; p. 46, bottom: © Claire Dibble; p. 47: © Robert E. Barber / Alamy; p. 48: Courtesy of Fairmont Hotels & Resorts; p. 49: © John E Marriott / All Canada Photos / SuperStock; p. 51: © Claire Dibble; p. 52, top: © Andrew Hempstead; p. 52, bottom: © Andrew Hempstead; p. 53: © Andrew Hempstead; p. 54, top: © Claire Dibble; p. 54, bottom: © Andrew Hempstead; p. 55: © Photo Don Lee, courtesy of the Banff Centre; p. 57, top: © Claire Dibble; p. 57, bottom: © Claire Dibble; p. 59: © Claire Dibble; p. 61: © Andrew Hempstead; p. 62: Courtesy Fairmont Hotels & Resorts; p. 63: © Claire Dibble; p. 65: © Claire Dibble; p. 66, top: © Andrew Hempstead; p. 66, bottom: © Claire Dibble; p. 67: © Darwin Wiggett / All Canada Photos / Alamy; p. 69: Courtesy Maple Leaf Grill & Lounge; p. 70: © Andrew Hempstead; p. 71, top: Courtesy of Fairmont Hotels & Resorts; p. 71, bottom: Courtesy Rimrock Resort Hotels; p. 72: © Andrew Hempstead; p. 73: Courtesy Maple Leaf Grill & Lounge; p. 74: © Photo by Heather McCoy, Courtesy Nourish; p. 75, top: Courtesy Wild Flour Bakery; p. 75, bottom: Courtesy Saltlik; p. 77: © Photo by Paul Zizka, Courtesy Num-Ti-Jah Lodge; p. 78: © Andrew Hempstead; p. 79: Courtesy of Fairmont Hotels & Resorts; p. 80: Courtesy of Fairmont Hotels & Resorts; p. 81, top: © Andrew Hempstead; p. 81, bottom: Courtesy of Banff Lodging Co.; p. 82, top: Courtesy Post Hotel & Spa; p. 82, bottom: Courtesy Rimrock Resort Hotels; p. 83: © Claire Dibble; p. 85: © Andrew Hempstead; p. 86: © Claire Dibble; p. 87: © Claire Dibble; p. 88: © Claire Dibble; p. 89: © Photo by Donald Lee, Courtesy of The Banff Centre; p. 90: Courtesy Aurora Nightclub; p. 91: © Claire Dibble; p. 93, top: © Andrew Hempstead; p. 93, bottom: Courtesy Kananaskis Country Golf Course; p. 94: © Claire Dibble; p. 96, top: © Claire Dibble; p. 96, bottom: © Claire Dibble; p. 97: © Andrew Hempstead; p. 99: © Claire Dibble; p. 100, top: © Andrew Hempstead; p. 100, bottom: © Claire Dibble; p. 102, top: © Barbara Larmon Failing / Frommers.com Community; p. 102, bottom: Courtesy Canadian Rockies Hot Springs; p. 104, top: © Claire Dibble; p. 104, bottom: © Claire Dibble; p. 105: © Claire Dibble; p. 107: © John E Marriott / All Canada Photos / SuperStock ; p. 108: © Claire Dibble; p. 109: © Claire Dibble; p. 111, top: © Andrew Hempstead; p. 111, bottom: Courtesy Kootenay River Runners; p. 113, top: © Andrew Hempstead; p. 113, bottom: © Andrew Hempstead; p. 114, top: Courtesy Kootenay Park Lodge; p. 114, bottom: © Claire Dibble; p. 115: © Claire Dibble; p. 117, top: © Claire Dibble; p. 117, bottom: © Andrew Hempstead; p. 118, top: © Claire Dibble; p. 118, bottom: Courtesy River Café; p. 119: Courtesy Calgary Stampede; p. 121: © Claire Dibble; p. 123: © Andrew Hempstead; p. 124: © Andrew Hempstead; p. 125, top: © Andrew Hempstead; p. 125, bottom: Courtesy Kensington Riverside Inn; p. 127, top: © Andrew Hempstead; p. 127, bottom: © Andrew Hempstead; p. 128: © Andrew Hempstead; p. 129: © Andrew Hempstead; p. 130, top: © Andrew Hempstead; p. 130, bottom: © Andrew Hempstead; p. 131: Courtesy Fairmont Hotels & Resorts; p. 132: © Andrew Hempstead; p. 133: © Claire Dibble; p. 135: Courtesy Horsethief Creek Pub; p. 136, top: Courtesy Kicking Horse Lodge; p. 136, bottom: Courtesy of Cathedral Mountain Lodge; p. 137: Courtesy Copper Horse Lodge; p. 138, top: Courtesy of Canadian Rocky Mountain Resorts; p. 138, bottom: Courtesy Lake O'Hara Lodge; p. 139: © Claire Dibble; p. 142: © Claire Dibble; p. 144, top: © Gerry M. Bates / Frommers.com Community; p. 144, bottom: © Andrew Hempstead; p. 145, top: © Claire Dibble; p. 145, bottom: © Andrew Hempstead; p. 147: © Claire Dibble; p. 148, top: © Claire Dibble; p. 148, bottom: © Claire Dibble; p. 149: © Claire Dibble; p. 151: © Claire Dibble; p. 152: © Claire Dibble; p. 153, top: © Craig Douce; p. 153, bottom: Courtesy Fairmont Hotels & Resorts; p. 154: © Claire Dibble; p. 155, top: © Andrew Hempstead; p. 155, bottom: © Claire Dibble; p. 157: Courtesy Banff Norquay; p. 158: © Photo by Sean Hannah, Courtesy Sunshine Village; p. 159: Courtesy Fairmont Hotels & Resorts; p. 160, top: © Ryan Creary / All Canada Photos / Alamy; p. 160, bottom: Courtesy Fairmont Hotels & Resorts; p. 161: © Andrew Hempstead.